Preposterous
Proverbs

Preposterous Proverbs

Why fine words butter no parsnips

Max Cryer

EXISLE
PUBLISHING

First published 2011

Exisle Publishing Limited,
P.O. Box 60-490, Titirangi, Auckland 0642, New Zealand.
'Moonrising', Narone Creek Road, Wollombi, NSW 2325, Australia.
www.exislepublishing.com

National Library of New Zealand Cataloguing-in-Publication Data

Cryer, Max.
Preposterous proverbs : why fine words butter no parsnips /
Max Cryer.
Includes bibliographical references.
ISBN 978-1-921497-45-2
1. Proverbs. I. Title.
398.9—dc 22

10 9 8 7 6 5 4 3 2 1

Text design and production by IslandBridge
Cover design by Christabella Designs
Printed in Singapore by KHL Printing Co Pte Ltd

This book uses paper sourced under ISO 14001 guidelines
from well-managed forests and other controlled sources.

Contents

Acknowledgements

The author particularly thanks Ian Watt, and also Graeme and Valerie Fisher, Geoffrey Pooch, Robbie Ancell, Joe Gilfillan, Nigel Horrocks, Steve Jennings, Paul Barrett, Graeme Hill and David Stevens.

Introduction

What is a proverb?

It's a tricky thing to define – there are so many variables. However, perhaps this is a fair description:

> *Proverb: an expression which, in a few words, encapsulates a perceived piece of analysis or advice which is applicable within a particular cultural context, and regarded as wisdom through having been entrenched in usage for many years.*

But can we feel sure that everything called a proverb can actually be regarded as 'wisdom'? Only sometimes. 'All that glisters is not gold.'

Can't argue with that.

However, other pithy quips identified as proverbs have less traction, and can be downright dodgy. Sometimes their wisdom might have worked well in a bygone era, but time has not treated them kindly. In the cold clear light of the 21st century, the advice given in some proverbs is open to question. For example:

'A dog, a woman, and a walnut tree,
The more you beat them the better they be.'

And these days the camera certainly can lie.

There is also an alarming number of proverbs which blatantly contradict each other. Take your pick:

'Birds of a feather flock together'

but

'Opposites attract.'

And is

'Out of sight out of mind'?

or does

'Absence make the heart grow fonder'?

(A 20th century update also exists: 'Absence makes the heart grow fonder – for somebody else.')

Then there are the head-scratching proverbs. What can these examples possibly mean?

'A dead bee maketh no honey.'

'A green yule makes a fat churchyard.'

'An apple, an egg and a nut, you may eat after a slut.'

Does a cat really have nine lives? No it doesn't. But undoubtedly there must once have been some reasoning behind the observation.

For several thousand years proverbs have been spoken in a portentous tone, chiselled into marble, embroidered by Jane Austen heroines onto framed linen or posted on handsome internet greetings. The very word itself summons involuntary respect, in spite of the difficulty in defining exactly what it is. But in addition, some pithy epigrams of 'perceived wisdom' have gathered around the margins of the usual definition of 'proverb'. Quotes and slogans, old wives' tales and catchphrases – even something as simple as the title of a successful book (e.g. *Life Begins at Forty*) have come into common usage and gained a kind of fragile truth, even if lacking the implied moral authority of traditional historic wisdom.

The present collection scratches the surface of several hundred proverbs, both familiar and obscure, and also includes some adages, maxims and epigrams which have crept into consideration – newcomers on the block which carry a certain illusion of inherent advice, albeit sometimes of questionable basis. We take a close look at just how relevant they really are.

And remember:

'If you would avoid suspicion, do not lace your shoes in a melon field.'

Yeah, right.

Max Cryer

'A proverb is to speech
what salt is to food.'

(Arabia)

Birth

**'We brought nothing into the world
and it is certain we carry nothing out.'**

(1 Timothy 6: 7)

It's difficult to believe that anyone took seriously the ancient verse:

**'Born on Monday fair of face,
Born on Tuesday full of grace
Born on Wednesday sour and sad,
Born on Thursday merry and glad,
Born on Friday worthily given,
Born on Saturday work for a living,
Born on Sunday never know want.'**

A cheerful piece of advice comes from Haiti:

'A monkey never thinks her baby is ugly.'

**'When the mouse has had
its fill, the meal turns bitter.'**
(Holland)

In Korea they assess the baby in a different way:

'A newborn baby has no fear of tigers.'

Africans confront a biological problem:

**'She who gives birth to triplets cannot ask
for a third breast.'**

And in Morocco the concern is for the vegetable garden:

**'The pumpkin gives birth and the fence
has the problem.'**

While Bulgarians are both pragmatic and fatalist:

**'Give me luck at my birth, then if you will –
throw me on the rubbish.'**

But while the Haitians may be cheerful and the Bulgarians pragmatic, some, including the Corsicans, view birth with a sense of deep gloom:

'At birth your fate is written.'

**'Do not use paper
to wrap up fire.'**
(China)

The Arabs agree:

> 'Only three things in life are certain – birth, death and change.'

And for the really gloomy, in 1660 the Rev. T. Fuller reminded us:

> 'Birth is the beginning of death.'

The German philosopher Arthur Schopenhauer was hardly optimistic in 1840:

> 'After your death, you will be what you were before birth.'

At least George Santayana could see some light in 1922:

> 'There is no cure for birth and death except for the interval between.'

'Painted flowers
have no scent.'
(Holland)

Take your pick

St Matthew records Jesus as saying:

'Ask and it shall be given to you.'

(Matthew 7: 7)

In 1738, Jonathan Swift was more cynical:

'The devil made askers.'

'He that would avoid old age
must hang himself in youth.'
(Yiddish)

Breeding

Nature or nurture? Nuggets of 'wisdom' exist in most cultures, but together they form a confusing jumble of contradictions about the comparative importance of inheritance and behaviour.

Euripides was confident that

'Noble fathers have noble children.'

Those who agreed with him echoed the thought:

'Like breeds like'

which then became:

'Like father, like son.'

'A girl with cotton stockings never sees a mouse.'
(USA)

But some eighteen hundred years later, Noah Webster pointed out that

'A good cow may have a bad calf'

and traditional Scottish wisdom formed an optimistic *opposite* impression:

'An ill cow may have a good calf.'

Sticking with the farmyard metaphor is the old favourite:

'There is a black sheep in every flock'

and Native Americans have long held that

'Not every sweet root gives birth to sweet grass.'

So it's clear that 'Like father, like son' is not a universal truth.

'A fog cannot be dispelled by a fan.'
(Japan)

Arguments still fly either way. Do children follow the precepts, values and characteristics of their antecedents, or do circumstances and contexts contribute to the make-up of individuals who might not exactly reflect their parents?

Paroemiologia Anglo-Latina proclaimed in 1639:

'Birth is much …but breeding is more.'

So possibly children *don't* necessarily reflect their parents' characteristics. Since 1460 we've been told instead that

'Manners make the man'

which seems to eliminate birth as a deciding factor. But more than 200 years later Thomas Fuller revised this to:

'Manners and money make a gentleman.'

From the Bible we learn that

'A tree is known by its fruit.' (Luke 6: 44)

Does this mean that people are judged by the way their children behave, or that children are judged by the reputation of their parents?

'A white glove often
conceals a dirty hand.'
(Italy)

While on the subject of fruit and breeding, another way of saying 'Like father, like son' is:

'An apple never falls far from the tree.'

This doesn't fit at all well with those maxims which favour the black sheep theory. Apples always fall directly downwards because of gravity, directly under the tree on which they were hanging. Growing and flourishing in that situation is unlikely, as soil is already occupied by roots underneath and light blocked by branches above. An apple which *rolls* away from the parent tree has a greater chance of flourishing, but apparently this is not what the proverb wants us to think.

'The sun loses nothing by shining into a puddle.'
(England)

How long does it take to make a gentleman? Chinese wisdom has it that

'One generation opens the road upon which another generation travels.'

In 1598, *Romei's Courtier's Academy* defined the time limit:

'It takes three generations to make a gentleman.'

Presumably the 'Like father, like son' factor applies for the first two of these generations.

But even so, things aren't always straightforward. A Lancashire proverb says that even if a family moves up from poor circumstances, the rise will be temporary – followed by a fall back to where they came from:

'Clogs to clogs in three generations.'

However, this doesn't seem to have applied to the Kennedys, Windsors, Rockefellers and Rothschilds.

'A serpent, though put in a bamboo tube, cannot crawl straight.'
(Korea)

'It runs in the blood like wooden legs.'

This Cheshire proverb appears to mean that not every fault of character can be blamed on one's genes – just as an amputated leg isn't hereditary.

Can a polished appearance, expensive tailoring and fine grooming give a semblance of good breeding? Not according to an Argentinian proverb which appeared in English in 1639:

'It is not the fine coat that makes the gentleman.'

In Spain, it is said of anyone overly conscious of an elegant background that:

'A man who prides himself on his ancestry is like a potato – the best part is under ground.'

'The shoe knows whether the sock has holes.'
(Germany)

Since 1594, cynical observers have noted that

> **'The higher the baboon climbs, the more
> undesirable are the parts exposed.'**

And in Mexico the message is blunt:

> **'Virtue is not inherited.'**

However, British clergyman John Ray confronted
believers in fine breeding with the ultimate put-down
in 1737:

> **'You come of good blood – but so does
> a black pudding.'**

'The sun shines on dung
but is not tainted.'
(Greece)

Oddities

'Judge not a man by his mother's words
... listen to his neighbours.'

'When the elephant sinks into the pit,
even the frog gives him a backward kick.'

'Many can drive an ox ... few can plough.'

'A nobleman, though drowning,
would never dog-paddle.'

'The swamp stands aloof as if
not related to the river.'

'It is safe to lend barley to him
who has oats.'

'Many a scoundrel marries not for
the sheep but for the wool.'

'The sleeping shrimp is carried away
with the current.'

'All ask if a man be rich,
none ask if he be good.'

'Eggs must not quarrel with stones.'

'Mediocrity means climbing molehills
without sweating.'

'Man's mind is a watch
which needs winding up daily.'

'He who has lost his oxen is
always hearing bells.'

'Every path has its puddle.'

Life

Patrick Dennis's fictional Aunty Mame (1958) had a firm belief:

> '**Life is a banquet – and most sons of bitches are starving.**'

And there are some who follow Walter B. Pitkin's 1932 decree that

> '**Life begins at forty.**'

So did the previous 39 years not count? Suspended animation perhaps ...

'The well-fed
have no religion.'
(Kashmir)

In 1553, Thomas Wilson's *The Art of Rhetoric* commented on the quality of life:

'They liued long enough, that have liued well enough.'

And Scottish essayist William Drummond condensed the matter in *A Midnight's Trance* (1619):

'Who liueth well, liueth long.'

The 'modern' version emerged in the Rev. T. Fuller's *The Holy State and the Profane State* (1642):

'He lives long that lives well.'

But can you rely on that?

Cervantes had disagreed in *Don Quixote* (1605):

'He that lives long suffers much.'

And Henry Bohn (1885) agreed with Cervantes:

'They seldom live well who think they shall live long.'

'A needle is sharp only at one end.'
(China)

William Wager, however, had disagreed all along, and in c.1569 published a book with a title declaring his belief:

'The longest thou livest the more foole thou art.'

While British folklore since 1678 has reminded everyone that the chores still have to be done:

'They that live longest must go farthest for wood.'

'As his name is, so is he.'

Although this has the might of the Bible behind it (1 Samuel 25: 25), it must be difficult to know how to interpret it if you have an ordinary name like Fred or Sue.

'Even a white lily casts a black shadow.'
(Hungary)

An ancient Latin maxim pronounces sternly on the continuance of life:

**'He is unworthy of life that gives no life
to another.'**

This appears to criticise voluntary celibacy (Roman Catholic nuns and priests, for example). But it seems rather harsh on those men and women who bitterly regret not being able to have children through no fault of their own.

**'A blind man cannot
judge colours.'**
(Geoffrey Chaucer)

Take your pick

You may be inclined to believe that

'Slow and steady wins the race'

but remember also that

'Time waits for no man.'

'An onion will not
produce a rose.'

(Italy)

32

What Makes a Man?

Appius Caecus (312 BC) believed that

> **'Every man is the architect of his own fortune.'**

But the God-fearing thought otherwise:

> **'Man proposes, God disposes.'**

In 1860 Wendell Phillips advised:

> **'Our self-made men are the glory of our institution.'**

'The son thinks he is one
month older than the father.'
(Burma)

But John Bright in 1868 disagreed – at least when describing Disraeli:

> **'He is a self-made man and worships his creator.'**

Cicero believed that

> **'A man is least known to himself'**

but *Paroemiologia Anglo-Latina* (1639) saw things differently:

> **'Every man is best known to himself'**

while a Yiddish proverb attests that

> **'Everyone sees his best friend in the mirror.'**

> 'It is easy to threaten a bull from a window.'
> (Italy)

The Chinese say:

> 'Everyone rakes the fire under his own pot.'

They also say:

> 'Behind an able man there are always other able men.'

Ancient Rome warned against too much self-satisfaction:

> 'He who is in love with himself need fear no rival'

and Lyly's *Euphues* (1589) advised modesty with

> 'Let your head be not higher than your hat.'

'Tomorrow will have the
same sun and moon as today.'
(West Africa)

'I think, therefore I am.'

So said French mathematician and philosopher Rene Descartes in 1637. His epigram implies that because he is capable of thinking – as we all are – then he is somehow better and more valuable than a massive oak tree, a beautiful orchid or the Victoria Falls, which all obey some form of control beyond our understanding. Dogs, elephants, cats, pandas and crocodiles – in fact all other creatures possess some form of mental activity. So like Descartes, they 'are'. (It's a bit hard to ascribe mental activity to a goldfish, but there's no doubt that they exist: they 'are'.)

Self-importance gets an even greater boost from the words of Greek philosopher Protagoras (c. 450 BC):

'Man is the measure of all things.'

'Every tub must stand on its own bottom.'

(England)

'Great minds think alike.'

Maybe, but not always. The leaders of any two opposing political parties may each be a 'great mind' – but do they think alike? Never. Let's not forget that most wars are based on the exact opposite to this proverb – that great minds usually think very differently before a conflict.

German philosopher Friedrich Nietzsche's supreme optimism in 1888 gave rise to:

'That which does not destroy me makes me stronger.'

This appears to overlook the fact that dire misfortune – air crashes, insurrections, riots and wars – can cause people physical and emotional damage which can cloud the rest of their lives.

'If your eye is sore, only
ever wipe it with your elbow.'
(Portugal)

The Chinese believe a nickname is an asset:

> 'If a man has no nickname he never
> grows rich'

but English essayist William Hazlitt, writing in 1821, didn't agree:

> 'A nickname is the hardest stone the Devil
> can throw at a man.'

An old Boston proverb surfaced in 1956:

> 'Don't get mad, get even.'

Expressing himself more mildly, C.S. Lewis agreed:

> 'Everyone says forgiveness is lovely until they
> have something to forgive.'

> 'A chip on the shoulder
> indicates wood higher up.'
> (Yiddish)

A Yiddish proverb warns that success isn't always easy to attain:

'The door to success is marked "push" and also "pull".'

Romanians have a retort for anyone even a little bit pretentious:

'You're a lady, I'm a lady – who will feed the pigs?'

The famous Dutch philosopher Desiderius Erasmus (c.1509) proclaimed:

'Fortune favours the fool.'

Three centuries later P.G. Wodehouse told us that Bertie Wooster agreed:

'Providence looks after all the chumps of this world.'

'A whore in a fine dress is like
a dirty house with a clean door.'
(Scotland)

For those who achieve greatness or have it thrust upon them, Thomas Fuller in 1732 advised that

'He who puts on a public gown must part with the private person'

while a saying from ancient Rome observed that

'Even for the wise the desire for glory is the last of all passions to be laid aside.'

Scottish wisdom came up with the most concise description:

'Egotism is an alphabet of one letter.'

And what of our place in the cosmos? In the Bible (Hebrews 2: 7) we are confidently told that

'Thou hast made him a little lower than the angels.'

'Words are good, but fowls lay eggs.'
(Germany)

Pope Xystus I (c. AD 120) was even more generous:

> **'Man is more precious in the sight of God than the angels'**

but St Bernard (patron saint of wax-melters) definitely didn't agree (c.1140):

> **'Man is nothing else than a sack of dung, the food of worms.'**

Shakespeare's Hamlet (and the musical *Hair* which quoted him) preferred a vaguely complimentary but non-committal middle ground:

> **'What a piece of work is a man.'**

'No flies alight on a boiling pot.'
(Spain)

Take your pick

'Might makes right.'

or

'Softly softly catchee monkey.'

'It is folly to sing
twice to a deaf man.'
(Denmark)

Solitude and Patience

Italians are gregarious:

'Solitude is intolerable, even in Paradise.'

But Arabian wisdom supports self-sufficiency:

'Solitude is better than bad company.'

Joseph Conrad in *Heart of Darkness* (1902) seemed to think we don't have a choice:

'We live as we dream – alone.'

'He who cannot dance
puts the blame on the floor.'
(Hindu)

In general, our understanding of the word 'patience' matches the opinion of the 16th century French statesman and essayist Michel de Montaigne, who in 1588 said simply:

> **'A man must learn to endure that patiently which he cannot conveniently avoid.'**

Over a century later, Lord Lansdowne agreed in his play *Heroic Love* (1696):

> **'Patience is the virtue of an ass that trots beneath his burden and is quiet.'**

Shakespeare had also used the four-legged image:

> **'Though patience be a tired mare, yet she will plod.'** *(Henry V)*

'A fallen tree does
not yield fruit.'
(Korea)

But by the time of Sir Walter Scott a certain cynicism had set in:

> **'Patience is a good nag, but she'll bolt.'**
>
> (*Woodstock*, 1826)

A dissenting voice came from author and bibliographer Henry George Bohn in 1855:

> **'He preacheth patience who never knew pain.'**

But Miguel Cervantes (1615) took a more generous view with his striking image:

> **'Patience is the plaster for all sores.'**

> **'A bald head is soon shaven.'**
>
> (Germany)

Take your pick

In the first century BC, Roman writer Lucretius decreed that 'quod ali cibus est aliis fuat acre venenum', which in 1604 became the English saying:

'One man's meat is another man's poison.'

But John Heywood had already expressed a contrary view in 1546, with 'As well for the coowe as for the bull.' This statement on the genders gradually became:

'What's good for the goose is good for the gander.'

'A goose drinks as much as a gander.'
(Denmark)

Silence

To speak or not to speak? For many centuries there has been wide dissension and inconsistent advice on the subject.

Persian wise men decreed:

'God protects the silent men.'

But *The Fontaine Fables* in 1671 felt sure that

'Silent people are dangerous.'

In ancient Greece people aligned themselves with the deities:

'Let me be silent, for so are the gods.'

But Sanskrit wisdom offered a less attractive opinion:

'Silence is the ornament of the illiterate.'

'Caesar has no authority over the grammarians.'
(Italy)

Francis Bacon agreed:

'Silence is the virtue of fools.'

Thomas Fuller, in *Gnomologia* (1732), took a more benign view:

'Silence seldom hurts.'

The most famous saying of all on this subject has its kernel as far back as the ancient Egyptians, who were known to believe that

'Silence is more profitable than abundance of speech.'

After passing through the Judaic Bible, this eventually caught the eye of historian and philosopher Thomas Carlyle who, in *Sartor Resartus* (1831), introduced the concept in German, accompanied by an English translation:

'Sprechen ist silbern, Schweigen ist golden.'

'Speech is silver, silence is golden.'

Commercial radio stations would not agree.

'He who knows the
road can ride full trot.'

(Italy)

Sometimes animals have been drawn into the argument. From ancient Europe comes:

'A shut mouth catches no flies.'

While in Korea they say:

'Even a fish wouldn't get into trouble if it kept its mouth shut.'

'To know is easier than to do.'
(Germany)

But the 'Don't talk' faction can still disagree with the 'Speak your mind' group. From Spain:

> **'Beware of the dog that does not bark and the man who does not talk.'**

West Africa, Germany and Ireland offer contrary opinions:

> **'There is nothing better for man than silence.'**

> **'A silent man is seldom ridiculed for his thoughts.'**

> **'A quiet tongue shows a wise head.'**

And still they come:

> **'Not to speak is the flower of wisdom.'**
> (Japan)

> **'Don't talk unless you can improve the silence.'**
> (America)

> **'Everyone is wise until he speaks.'**
> (Ireland)

> **'A fool who can keep silent is counted among the wise.'**
> (Yiddish)

> **'A man is as old as his feet.'**
> (USA)

'Give your ears to words but do not give your words to ears.'

(India)

'A bridle for the tongue is a necessary piece of furniture.'

(China)

'The tongue is the neck's worst enemy.'

(Egypt)

But a saw from Holland takes a firmly alternate view:

'I have a mouth which I feed, it must speak what I please.'

'Donkeys' lips don't fit onto a horse's mouth.'

(China)

Voltaire famously declared:

> '**I may disagree with what you have to say,
> but I shall defend to the death your right
> to say it.**'

And Dr Samuel Johnson followed up with:

> '**Every man has the right to utter what he
> thinks truth, and every other man has
> the right to knock him down for saying it.**'

Speaking what you please can involve harsh or wounding comments, bringing varying outcomes. It is generally agreed that this Spanish proverb is correct:

> '**A word and a stone thrown can never
> be recalled.**'

> '**An unlucky person falls on
> his back and bruises his nose.**'
> (Yiddish)

But do harsh words leave a lasting effect? Yiddish wisdom says:

> 'The smart of a blow subsides, the sting of a word abides.'

The Turks agree:

> 'A knife wound heals, a wound from words does not.'

But Italians are more dismissive:

> 'Hard words break no bones.'

And whether silver or golden, a proverb presented by Erasmus in 1539 has scant use nowadays:

> 'Silence is the best ornament of a woman.'

Thomas Fuller rephrased the sentiment two centuries later in his *Gnomologia*:

> 'Silence is a fine Jewel for a Woman … but it is little worn.'

'Salt never calls itself sweet.'
(Germany)

Take your pick

If advised to

'Strike while the iron is hot'

remember also that

'Haste makes waste.'

**'It is no use making
shoes for geese.'**
(Denmark)

Truth

A German proverb opines that

> **'Truth is to the ears what smoke is to the eyes and vinegar to the teeth.'**

Hindus don't agree:

> **'Truth is sweeter than sugar.'**

Lord Byron said in 1823:

> **'Truth is stranger than fiction.'**

Sometimes this is the case, but Byron hadn't read *The Lord of the Rings*. Nor was he put to the test of assessing whether truth was stranger than Spiderman, Alice in her rabbit-hole, Harry Potter, the Incredible Hulk ...

'Always keep your shoes on when treading on thorns.'
(Hebrew)

German wisdom says:

'An old error is always more popular than a new truth.'

This is often the case. There is no evidence that Queen Victoria said 'We are not amused', lemmings do not throw themselves into the sea, ostriches do not bury their heads in the sand, and Conan Doyle never wrote the line 'Elementary, my dear Watson.' But these misbeliefs are much cherished.

'If my aunt had been a man she'd be my uncle.'
(England)

An old proverb says:

'A lie can go round the world and back while truth is lacing up its boots.'

This was remarkably prescient of whoever created the adage, which apparently pre-dates 1859 (when it was first acknowledged). At that time nobody really knew the full extent of 'the world', and later inventions made a lie move even faster: satellite telephony, the internet, e-mail, Twitter and other forms of rapid transmission of information and misinformation, gossip and scandal.

'A spot shows most on the finest cloth.'
(Spain)

'Time will tell.'

It hasn't yet told about Stonehenge, the Pyramids, Atlantis or Easter Island.

Tell the truth or not? An old piece of Yiddish advice has it that you

'Tell the truth and you ask for a beating'

but the Slavic nations have the last word:

'Speak the truth but leave immediately.'

'A used plough shines, standing water stinks.'

(Germany)

Clothes

There is alarming disparity among proverbs and maxims concerning the importance of what we wear.

Erasmus told us in 1533 that

> 'Clothes make the man.'

Which by 1591 began to change:

> 'Apparel makes the man.'

> 'The tailor makes the man.'

While from Wales comes the assurance that

> 'Becoming clothes are two-thirds of beauty.'

'Do not wade where you can't see the bottom.'
(Denmark)

To some, the outward look of a person provides sufficient evidence to judge them. Italian wisdom is more cautious:

'Appearances are deceitful.'

And in *The Pilgrim's Progress* (1678), John Bunyan offered the classic line:

'Fine feathers that make a fine bird.'

This originated from an observation by Stefano Guazzo in 1574 that while a peacock is splendid in full display, when plucked and laid out next to a turkey carcass there is little or no difference between the two. So the peacock's fine feathers make an impressive show, but don't reflect any particular quality in the bird beneath. The message seems to be that no matter what you wear, your personal values and family background – whether elegant or shabby – will eventually break through your sartorial image.

'Dirty water will quench fire.'
(Italy)

Assuming that silk and ermine are worn by the rich and privileged, and scarlet is the colour of cardinals and princes, then beware that

> 'In silk and scarlet walks many a harlot'

and

> 'An ape's an ape, a varlet's a varlet,
> though they be clad in ermine and scarlet'

and

> 'Reynard is still Reynard tho' he put
> on a cowl.'

Playwright John Heywood, in *Royal King and Loyal Subject* (1603), showed scant regard for either breeding or buying off the peg with

> 'It takes nine tailors to make a man.'

And Benjamin Franklin is credited with saying in 1758:

> 'Silks and satins, scarlet and velvets,
> put out the kitchen fire.'

'Exaggeration is to paint
a snake ... then add legs.'
(China)

In other words, for the sake of wearing finery, people have gone with a hungry belly and half-starved their families. He explained:

'These are not the necessaries of life; they can scarcely be called the conveniences; and yet, only because they look pretty, how many want to have them! By these, and other extravagances, the genteel are reduced to poverty, and forced to borrow.'

Fashion and apparel form a huge industry aimed especially at women. According to some ancient Romans, only women need bother about 'becoming' clothes. They believed that fashion and grooming aimed at the male market achieved little purpose, because:

'Neglect of appearance is becoming in men.'

Perhaps they foresaw today's designer stubble and distressed denim.

'A vessel holds only its fill.'
(Ireland)

Three nations with varying wisdom about style:

'Good clothes open all doors.'

(Germany)

'What's in fashion will go out of fashion.'

(Japan)

While from France (curiously):

'Fools invent fashion and wise men follow them.'

'A full cup must be carried steadily.'

(Scotland)

Take your pick

Johann Wolfgang von Goethe said in 1774:

**'The best pleasures of this world
are not quite good.'**

A generation earlier, in 1739, King Frederick
the Great of Prussia said:

**'Pleasure is the most real good
in this life.'**

'A handsaw is a good thing
– but not to shave with.'

(England)

Face and Hair

Decimus Iunius Iuvenalis (Juvenal for short) was a Roman poet active in the early part of the 2nd century AD, and not known for his kindness. He observed, quite rightly:

> **'Your face counts your years.'**

It is doubtful that many contemporary film stars would agree. The Oscar ceremony red carpet may better reflect another proverb originated by Pierre Corneille in 1642:

> **'The face is often only a smooth imposter.'**

'What is done by night appears by day.'
(Romania)

But an olive branch was extended by famous French poet Jean de la Fontaine, who decreed in *The Heron and the Damsel* (1671):

'The ruins of a house may be repaired – why cannot those of a face?'

Cue applause from a thousand cosmetic surgeons.

A German offering was more forthright:

'On a wrinkled neck, a pearl weeps.'

But who else can afford them?

One of the more bizarre decrees of 'wisdom' about the face is from Oxfordshire folklore:

'If you have a vein across your nose, You'll never live in wedding clothes.'

Which is depressing as well as nonsensical.

'He must stoop that hath a low door.'
(England)

As far back as the 1500s there are references to the futility of damaging part of the face to make a point about something less important. Two hundred years later the concept had developed into:

'Don't cut off your nose to spite your face.'

Obviously this is intended to be a metaphor: 'Don't do anything rash and spectacular which could affect the positive aspects of a bigger issue.' However, there has been a massive change of direction in the image on which it is based. These days, many an ill-shaped nose has been decreed as career-limiting and given to a surgeon to improve ... hopefully to improve the face rather than spite it.

The nose also figured in an old belief with many bizarre versions, the most absurd of which was highlighted in Jonathan Swift's *Polite Conversation* (1738):

'If your nose itches you will shake hands with a fool.'

'Mountains live longer than kings.'
(Holland)

Beauty and its value are sometimes bracketed, as in this pragmatic 17th century Dutch proverb:

> **'Beauty is potent but Money is omnipotent.'**

While Yiddish humour determines bluntly that

> **'A pretty face costs money.'**

The Japanese acknowledge the attraction of youth with the cynical observation:

> **'Even the Devil was handsome at eighteen.'**

British romantic poet John Keats believed that

> **'Beauty is truth and truth beauty.'**

But both halves of this equation may be doubtful ...

> **'He that sings on Friday will weep on Sunday.'**
> (England)

From Morocco comes a mother-in-law's put-down:

**'My daughter-in-law is beautiful ...
but don't look any deeper.'**

In 1608, British dramatist John Day (in *Law Tricks*)
announced that

'A good face needs no paint.'

Millions of the world's women demonstrate the truth
of this, but they are rewarded by being referred to as
from 'undeveloped nations'. In the 'developed' world,
the multi-billion-dollar cosmetics industry does not
want anyone to acknowledge even one grain of truth
in John Day's belief – and would prefer it were never
mentioned.

**'God can shave
without soap.'**
(Poland)

Shakespeare's *Venus and Adonis* endorsed dimples:

'Love made these hollows.'

But the Irish showed gloomy suspicion:

'A dimple on the cheek – a devil within.'

'The only honest miller is
the one with hair on his teeth.'

(Germany)

To have or not to have?

'A hairy man is a lucky man.'

(Spain)

'Curly hair, curly thoughts.'

(Russia)

From Greece comes the observation:

'Grey hair is a sign of age, but not wisdom.'

One survey reported that Americans spent $1.6 billion annually on hair colouring – because the grey *is* a sign of age. This is not the case in Spain, whence comes the proverb:

'Those who dye their hair fool only themselves.'

'Two daughters and a back door are three arrant thieves.'

(England)

Among the more arcane pieces of rhyming folklore is this warning about personal grooming from 17th century Devon:

'Sunday shaven, Sunday shorn –
Better hadst thou ne'er been born.'

This tired old rhyme has no connection with real life – and Gillette probably won't be using it as an advertising slogan.

'The moon shines
but it does not warm.'
(Ukraine)

1 Corinthians 11: 15 tells us:

> **'If a woman hath long hair it is a glory to her.'**

But a succinct French proverb begs to differ:

> **'Long hair – little sense.'**

Trust Germany to provide the eminently practical:

> **'Short hair is soon brushed.'**

But from Denmark comes a spot-on observation:

> **'A bad haircut is two people's shame.'**

'Every man must scratch his head with his own nails.'
(Arabia)

Take your pick

Confucius is credited with saying
this, c. 500 BC:

**'Music produces a kind of pleasure which
human nature cannot do without.'**

But in 1561 Welsh poet George Herbert
was not impressed:

'Music helps not the toothache.'

'The stars make no noise.'

(Ireland)

Tall or Short

Despite the lack of any scientific or sociological evidence either way, there is nevertheless abundant 'wisdom' about the perceived qualities of people according to their height.

Wise words about being tall are fairly rare – and curiously uncomplimentary. An ancient Hebrew proverb had set the ball rolling:

'Tall men had ever empty heads'

which found its way into antiquated English as:

'The longe man is seld wys.'

In 1562 John Heywood stuck the knife into tall people:

'Long be thy legs and short be thy life.'

'It is not easy to blow and swallow at the same time.'
[22 BC]

A similar sentiment is found in Tuscany:

> 'La casa grandi dal mezzo in su non s'abitano.'

The Spanish concurred:

> 'El grande de cuerpo no es muy hombre.'

What they're all saying is:

> 'The robust man is rarely a great man.'

A rather whimsical alternative version surfaced:

> 'Oftimes such as are built four storeys high are observed to have little in their cock-loft.'

This concept, which was already old, is reported to have had an airing in England around 1620 when King James I asked Sir Francis Bacon for his opinion on the new, and very tall, French ambassador. Bacon replied:

> 'Tall men are like houses of four or five storeys, wherein the upper room is worst furnished.'

> 'A man is truly stingy who gets only one measle at a time.'
>
> (Ireland)

On the other hand, proverbs have provided ample support for the vertically challenged. In 1611, lexicographer Randle Cotgrave opined:

> **'A little body doth often harbour a great soul.'**

Or, to express it rather differently:

> **'A little bush may hold a great hare.'**

Talking up short people occurs elsewhere:

> **'Little people have big hearts.'**
> (Germany)

> **'Men are not to be measured by inches.'**
> (England)

> **'Oaks may fall when reeds stand the storm.'**
> (England)

> **'The smallest axe may fell the hugest oak.'**
> (England)

> **'In the entire body of a big man, wisdom cannot cirulate.'**
> (Japan)

> **'He is guilty who is not at home.'**
> (Ukraine)

A dissenting voice can be found in Fuller's *Gnomologia* (1732), but it may have referred to just one known individual:

> 'He's a little fellow but every bit of that little is bad.'

A fine old standby is:

> 'Good things can come in small packages.'

But a corrupted version evolved over time:

> 'Good things can come in small packages … so does poison.'

China offers cryptic advice:

> 'When with dwarfs, do not talk about pygmies.'

But let's give Denmark the last word:

> 'A little dog, a cow without horns and a short man are generally proud.'

'If you put it in the tank
do not seek it in the well.'

(India)

Food

To meat or not to meat?

A Portuguese proverb says:

> 'Much meat – many maladies.'

Ancient Rome didn't agree:

> 'No man will feed on herbs when meat
> is to be had.'

Optimism can be found in *Heywood's Proverbs* (1546):

> 'God never sendeth mouth but he
> sendeth meat.'

'Abundance can make
cotton pull a stone.'
(Germany)

In 1542 a treatise called *Dyetary of Health* included a rather cryptic statement, which it referred to as 'an old proverb':

'God sends meat and the devil sends cooks.'

That 'old proverb' remained in circulation for several centuries, but was heard less frequently in the 20th century. Which may be just as well, since belief in its veracity would doubtless have carved holes in the cookbook publishing business and caused outrage to television cooks everywhere – perhaps even an entire Food Channel.

Ralph Waldo Emerson, when discussing excellence in 1841, used a dairy metaphor:

'Cream always rises to the top.'

Which is probably right – excellence does tend to show itself. But the metaphor hasn't worn well. In the 21st century cream seldom rises any more, since homogenisation eliminates the separation of cream

'What you can't have, abuse.'

(Italy)

from milk, except for cream that is collected and sold in separate bottles. No more rising to the surface ...

Charles Dickens in *Nicholas Nickleby* (1839) advised:

'Subdue your appetites and you've conquered human nature.'

Dickens would not find any support from the advertising industry, which strains every muscle to make sure we do *not* subdue our appetites. In the same way, the restaurant trade firmly disagrees with Benjamin Franklin's advice:

'To lengthen thy life, lessen thy meals.'

To eat or not to eat?

James Howell announced in 1659:

'Eat less and drink less and buy a knife at Michaelmas.'

Michaelmas is celebrated on 29 September, but the reason for buying a knife on that date is totally obscure.

'Dirt may stick to a mud wall but not to polished marble.'
(USA)

Lyly decreed in 1592:

'Eat enough and it will make you wise.'

A proverb from long ago advises:

'Often and little eating makes a man fat.'

But an old Italian saying supports regular eating:

'He who goes to bed supperless tosses all night.'

While Hindu wisdom tells us:

'Never be modest in eating or business.'

Two cultures with differing attitudes:

'Eat with him and beware of him.'
(Portugal)

'One is never well at table unless there be four in company.'
(Arabia)

'Deep swimmers and high climbers seldom die in their beds.'
(Holland)

> 'East is East and West is West
> And Never the Twain shall Meet.'

Does this mean that all the Chinese, Thai, Indian, Turkish, Korean and Taiwanese restaurants in Britain, the US, Australia and Africa don't actually exist?

John Clarke in 1639 published:

> 'You must eat a peck of ashes ere you die.'

A peck is approximately nine litres! Over time 'ashes' became 'dirt', and an alternative version (attributed to Lord Chesterfield) gained currency:

> 'We must all eat a peck of dirt before we
> die – but none of us wants it all at once.'

> 'An inch in a sword
> or a palm in a lance
> is a great advantage.'
> (Spain)

One curious saying is

'First catch your hare …'

In spite of rumours to the contrary, nobody knows how the term originated. The novelist William Thackeray used the line in 1855, but no evidence exists that Mrs Beeton or Hannah Glasse ever said it.

There are two notable pieces of wisdom about pies, the first from Russia:

'A kind word is better than a big pie.'

In England, James Howell's *Proverbs* in 1659 told us:

'He that hath eaten a bear pie will always smell of the garden.'

The dietary preference (a bear pie!) would be weird in itself, except that in some places 'bear pie' is a fanciful name for a lush dessert, often including broken

'The crow does not roost with the phoenix.'
(China)

biscuits of dark colour. Why it makes someone smell of the garden is unclear, for 'garden' appears to refer to London's 17th century 'Bear-garden', an outdoor arena built for animal sports such as bull-baiting and bear-baiting.

An ancient Cornish saying identifies someone who is less than acute:

'Went in with the loaves and came out with the cakes.'

Bread takes longer to bake than cakes, so this person is only 'half-baked' – not quite the full sandwich, one shingle short of a load, etc.

'Whatever is in the pot
will come out on the spoon.'
(Hindu)

Some slightly puzzling international maxims:

'He who has plenty of butter may put some on his cabbage.'

(Denmark)

'When the sea turned into honey the poor man lost his spoon.'

(Bulgaria)

'Eat coconuts while you have teeth.'

(Sri Lanka)

'Of all birds, give me mutton.'

(England, 1732)

'Will God's blessing make my pot boil?'

(Scotland)

'Worms eat a sour apple.'

(Poland)

'Though honey is sweet, don't lick it off a briar.'

(Ireland)

'An egg today is better than a chicken tomorrow.'

(Italy)

'Eagles fly alone but sheep flock together.'

(Scotland)

'He who eats his fowl alone must saddle his horse alone.'

(Spain)

'Who has a head of butter must not come near the oven.'

(Netherlands)

'Listen to conscience and you will have nothing to eat.'

(China)

'Eat the fruit and don't enquire about the tree.'

(Turkey)

'Everything has an end, except a sausage which has two.'

(Germany)

'Adam ate the apple and our teeth still ache.'

(Hungary)

And an old African-American prediction:

'Don't pour tea before first putting sugar in the cup, or someone will be drowned.'

'Never ask a barber if you need a haircut.'

(USA)

Oddities

'The peach will have wine,
and the fig water.'

'Crumb not your bread before
you taste your porridge.'

'Fine words butter no parsnips.'

'Boil stones in butter and you
may sip the broth.'

'You should eat a bushel of salt with
a man before you trust him.'

'Honey is not for the ass's mouth.'

'If you drink with your porridge
you'll cough in your grave.'

'If you eat a pudding at home,
the dog shall have the skin.'

'You can't hang soft cheese
on a hook.'

'It's a poor roast that gives
no dripping.'

'Meat and mass never hindered man.'

'He that eats less eats most.'

'He that eats until he is sick
must fast until he is well.'

'If you hate a man, eat his bread.
If you love him, do the same.'

The food's destination – the belly – comes in for some attention too:

'The belly has no ears.'

(England)

'The belly gives no credit.'

(Denmark)

'Spinach is the broom of the stomach.'

(France)

And Randle Cotgrave in 1611 announced what mothers have always known:

'A growing youth has a wolf in his belly.'

'The barking of a dog does
not disturb a man on a camel.'

(Egypt)

In 1529, a long-held belief first appeared in print:

'The moon is made of green cheese.'

The 'green' here refers not to a colour, but to 'green' as in young and not yet fully formed, so the pale yellowish colour of the moon seemed similar to newly made, not-matured (or green) cheese. (After 1969, there was no more doubt about what the moon was made of.)

Here are two obscure proverbs:

'A man of many trades begs his bread on Sundays.'

A somewhat mysterious way of confirming that it is difficult to have two jobs simultaneously.

Thomas Nashe's *Unfortunate Traveller* (1594) delivered the (very English) decree that

'Garlic makes a man wink, drink and stink.'

'Knotty timber requires hard wedges.'
(Romania)

We didn't know about the winking and drinking ... just the stink.

And Ireland combined whimsy and pragmatism with:

'You can't spoil a rotten egg.'

Thomas Percy's *Reliques of Ancient Poetry* (1765) records that

'The nearer the bone the sweeter the flesh.'

But 18th century Scots believed the opposite:

'The flesh is aye fairest that is farthest from the bone.'

However, there is a belief that this refers to women being more attractive when they're plump!

'The one who washes off dirt washes off luck.'
(Mongolia)

Finally, everyone knows that

'Many hands make light work.'

But don't forget the equally well-known:

'Too many cooks spoil the broth.'

'The doctor must heal
his own bald head.'
(Iran)

Take your pick

Like many subjects covered in proverbs, food 'wisdom' is often contradictory.

Roman lyric poet Horace in 23 BC assured his readers that

'Quid quisque vivet nunquam homini satis cautum est in horas.'

In other words:

'That which one most anticipates comes to pass.'

But English novelist Mrs Elizabeth Gaskell enunciated a far more widespread belief in *Mary Barton* (1848):

'A watched pot never boils.'

'Dogs have teeth in all countries.'
(Holland)

Wine and
Strong Drink

The Bible is very encouraging:

> **'Wine cheereth God and man.'**
>
> (Judges 9: 13)

And again:

> **'Wine maketh glad the heart of man.'**
>
> (Psalm 104: 15)

But a different view is expressed in Proverbs 20:1:

> **'Wine is a mocker, strong drink a brawler; and whosoever is deceived thereby is not wise.'**

'Don't sell the bear's skin before you enter the woods.'
(Yiddish)

Some later encouragement came in 1771 with this nod from John Wesley:

> **'Wine is one of the noblest cordials in nature.'**

And an impressive endorsement from eminent scientist Louis Pasteur in 1895:

> **'Wine is the most helpful and hygienic beverage.'**

But there have been plenty of dissenting voices throughout history. In 800 BC Homer was advising:

> **'Wine leads to folly.'**

And in c. AD 43, Seneca followed up with:

> **'Wine kindles wrath.'**

In his *Wits' Theatre* (1598), John Bodenham announced:

> **'Wine has drowned more men than the sea.'**

And Samuel Johnson delivered this blast in 1778:

> **'Wine gives a man nothing, neither knowledge nor wit.'**

'One cannot make soup out of beauty.'
(Estonia)

Koreans are equally cautious:

> 'A cup of wine is medicine, a gallon of
> wine is ruin.'

And a piece of advice which could only come from Japan:

> 'Man drinks wine, then wine drinks
> wine, then wine drinks man.'

Has a drunkard any form of control?

> 'The devil has no power over a drunkard.'

Nobody has any power over a drunkard. All entertainers know that an audience member who is drunk and disruptive cannot be reasoned with.

A piece of somewhat unwise advice from ancient French:

> 'If you would live forever you must
> wash the milk off your liver.'

From Yiddish folklore comes:

> 'The bar owner loves drunks, but not
> perhaps for a son-in-law.'

> 'Don't make an oven
> of your cap or a garden
> of your belly.'
> (France)

Oddities

Thomas Cogan's *The Haven of Health* (1588) put paid to an old and medically unsound belief by launching a proverbial paradox:

'Drink wine and have the gout;
Drink no wine and have the gout.'

It's true: a teetotaller can get gout.

From Russia comes this enigmatic thought:

'Vodka is the aunt of wine.'

And some possibly misplaced confidence from 1639:

'I know what I do when I drink.'

Most people find the reverse is true.

Somewhat quixotically, the Irish claim:

> **'A good drink ends in thirst.'**

But degeneration sets in:

> **'Ale in, wit out.'**

And the non-drinker observes:

> **'He that drinks beer thinks beer.'**

And finally, two pearls of Mediterranean wisdom:

> **'Water drinkers do not write songs.'**
>
> (Greece)

> **'He who drinks wine sleeps,
> he who sleeps does not sin,
> And he who does not sin
> goes straight to Heaven.'**
>
> (Spain)

**'Stay with your old shoes
until God provides new ones.'**
(Arabia)

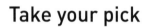

Take your pick

'Actions speak louder
than words'

or

'The pen is mightier
than the sword.'

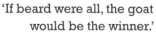

'If beard were all, the goat
would be the winner.'
(Denmark)

Women

For many centuries, the best-known philosophers, writers and purveyors of wisdom were men – and rather misogynist men at that, judging by much of the 'wisdom' they generated about women. In more recent times a rather warmer tone has emerged.

First, a selection of sayings which are really past their use-by date.

This little gem dates back to Gilbertus Cognatus's *Adagia* of 1629:

> **'A dog, a woman and a walnut tree –**
> **the more you beat them the better they be.'**

Don't even think about it. Except perhaps the tree – apparently it does encourage a more prolific production of nuts.

'A beautiful woman smiling
bespeaks a purse weeping.'
(Italy)

In 1570 it was okay to say:

> 'Deeds are males, words are females.'

Then from Thomas Fuller's collection in 1732:

> **Maidens must be mild and meek,**
> **Swift to hear and slow to speak.**

Don't tell Germaine Greer.

Benjamin Franklin had a sour view of a young woman's potential:

> **'An undutiful daughter will prove an unmanageable wife.'**

In Jamaica it is believed:

> **'A beautiful woman is a beautiful trouble.'**

While in ancient Portugal apparently they didn't like women too slim:

> **'A goose, a woman and a goat are bad things lean.'**

'Better to sit all night than
go to bed with a dragon.'
(China)

Internationally, there have been some less than flat-
tering proverbs:

'Women and hens are lost by too much
gadding about.'

(Italy)

'A woman's tongue is her sword and she
does not let it rust.'

(France)

'Many women means many words.'

(Kurdistan)

'All women are chaste where there are
no men.'

(Sanskrit)

'Between a woman's "yes" and "no" there
is no room for the point of a needle.'

(Germany)

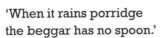

'When it rains porridge
the beggar has no spoon.'

(Denmark)

As for women staying at home, as early as 467 BC the Greek dramatist Aeschylus decreed in *Seven Against Thebes*:

> 'Let women stay at home and hold
> their peace.'

By 1732 Thomas Fuller had developed an English version of the theme in his *Gnomologia: Adagies and Proverbs*:

> 'A woman is to be from her house
> three times: when she is christened,
> married and buried.'

A century later (1832) the *Edinburgh Magazine and Literary Miscellany* urged:

> 'A woman's place is in the bosom
> of her family; her thoughts ought
> seldom to emerge from it.'

But these days, quote any of the above at your peril!

'If you marry the donkey
you must carry its load.'

(Iran)

The relationship between husband and wife has produced some strange images:

> 'When the mistress is the master,
> the parsley grows the faster.'

And

> 'Man is the head of the family; woman
> is the neck that turns the head.'

And inexplicably:

> 'Parsley fried will bring a man to his
> saddle and a woman to her grave.'

'There are more old
drunkards than old doctors.'
(France)

Less then perfect housewives and women of easy virtue also make an appearance:

'She cannot leap an inch from a slut.'

Here 'slut' means an untidy person. This is believed to be a 17th century put-down. The unfortunate woman thus described is untidy – so close to being an actual slut that she cannot pretend to be even one inch beyond that state.

And then there is this thinly disguised real estate metaphor from the 17th century:

'She lies backwards and lets out her fore-rooms.'

Referring, of course, to a woman with a generous disposition and few inhibitions about how to earn some funds with whatever facilities she has to offer.

John Florio's comment in 1591 may be a compliment – or is it?

'One hair of a woman draws more than a team of oxen.'

'A duck will not always dabble in the same gutter.'
(Denmark)

In 1970, Australian author, editor and documentary film-maker Irina Dunn, who was studying for an honours degree in language and literature, wrote on two Sydney doors:

**'A woman needs a man like a fish
needs a bicycle.'**

She later admitted to *Time* that she was being 'a bit of a smart-arse', but the expression spread like wildfire. In the US it quickly became a familiar part of the women's liberation movement.

**'A dress not worn
wears itself out.'**
(Armenia)

Oddities

'A dog's nose and a maid's knees
are always cold.'

(1639)

'Bare walls make giddy housewives.'

(1695)

'A wife is not a pot –
she will not break so easily.'

(Russia)

'Onions, smoke and a shrew make
a good man's eyes water.'

(Denmark)

'Among ten men, nine are sure
to be women.'

(Turkey)

'As great a pity to see a woman weep
as to see a goose go barefoot.'

(1526)

'As honest a woman as
ever burnt malt.'

(1589)

'Gaming, women and wine,
while they laugh, make men pine.'

(1640)

But there are some positives.

Yiddish belief is that

> 'God created woman from the rib
> of a man so that she should be
> near his heart.'

Friedrich Nietzsche was whole-hearted about it in *Thus Spake Zarathustra*:

> 'Happiness is a woman.'

The Spanish acknowledge a woman's support:

> 'A man with a good wife can bear any evil.'

In India a woman's presence supersedes physical looks:

> 'A wife gives beauty to a house.'

The Irish encourage couples:

> 'Tis a lonely washing that has no man's
> shirt in it.'

> 'The first breath you take
> is the beginning of death.'
> (England)

And misogynist wisdom has been banished by the Chinese, whose warm assessment is:

> 'A hundred men can make an encampment,
> but only a woman can make a home.'

And finally from Germany:

> 'A house without a woman is like
> a body without a soul.'

'You cannot go to
heaven unless you die.'
(India)

Take your pick

In *An Essay on Man* (1733), Alexander Pope declared:

**'Hope springs eternal in
the human breast.'**

But the Bible is markedly more pessimistic:

**'Hope deferred makes
the heart sick.'**

(Proverbs 13: 12)

**'A drowning man
reaches for his own hair.'**

(Greece)

Love

'Love can be afraid of nothing.'

(Seneca, c. AD 60)

Frank Sinatra might have convinced us that love and marriage go together like a horse and carriage, but according to the proverbs it isn't always that simple. To begin with, the state of love can affect cognitive function ...

Friedrich Nietzsche announced somewhat cynically:

'A pair of powerful spectacles has sometimes sufficed to cure a person in love.'

'Who is born of a hen, must scratch.'

(Italy)

And there is plenty of international agreement that love can daze the thinking:

'Affection is a bad judge.'

(Italy)

'Fire in the heart sends smoke into the head.'

(Germany)

'Love and blindness are twin sisters.'

(Russia)

'A man in love mistakes a pimple for a dimple.'

(Japan)

'A young man's love is water in a sieve.'

(Spain)

'He who falls in love meets a worse fate than he who leaps from a rock.'

(Italy)

'He who drinks on credit gets drunk in less time.'

(Armenia)

Love knows no seasons. The Danes say:

**'When the gorse is out of bloom,
kissing's out of fashion.'**

The French believe some separation stokes the fire:

'A fence between makes love more keen.'

But the pathway isn't always clear. In Sweden they have found:

**'Love is a dew which falls on both lilies
and nettles.'**

And tradition in Iran holds that

**'A broken hand works, but not a broken
heart.'**

**'More people drown
by drink than in water.'**
(Scotland)

'Virtue is its own reward.'

It's hard to work out if this applies to Mick Jagger, Rod Stewart, the President of Italy, Errol Flynn or Shane Warne.

A saying often repeated is that

'All the world loves a lover.'

And sometimes it's true – unless he/she is married to someone else. (Tiger Woods' sponsors didn't love him so much after his affairs were exposed.)

And it certainly isn't true that

'Love conquers all.'

In fiction it didn't work for Tristan and Isolde, Romeo and Juliet or Mimi and Rodolfo … and in real life not for Prince Charles and Diana.

Some don't stand up to scrutiny:

'None but the brave deserve the fair.'

That is something of an unwarranted slap in the face for the ordinary, law-abiding, happily married suburban couple.

'He who is a fool tries to drink with a fork.'
(China)

Oddities

'Love and a cough cannot be hid.'

(England)

'The greatest love is a mother's,
then a dog's, then a sweetheart's.'

(Poland)

'After being kissed by a rogue,
count your teeth immediately.'

(Hebrew)

'It is easy to halve the potato
where there's love.'

(Ireland)

(Presumably this refers to generosity
in times of adversity.)

Love in absentia

Almost half a century BC, the poet Sextus Aurelius Propertius penned a line about lovers being apart from each other:

'Semper in absentes felicior aestus amantes'

which, translated literally, means:

'Warmth between lovers is enhanced when they are apart.'

Greek philosophy tended to agree:

'From far away and beloved is better than close by and arguing.'

Fifteen hundred years after Sextus Aurelius's original statement, the sentiment filtered into English, eventually coming full circle in 1844 as:

'Absence makes the heart grow fonder.'

But the *Proverbs of* [King] *Alfred* (c. 1250) present a more cynical view:

'He that is ute bi-loken [shut out]

He is inne sone foryeten [forgotten].'

'The branch must be bent early that is to make a good crook.'
(Denmark)

A century later the Augustinian monk Thomas à Kempis stated:

> **'Whan Man is oute of sight, son be he passith oute of mynde.'**

Later, British poet Arthur Hugh Clough provided a more concise summary:

> **'Out of sight, out of mind.'**

It achieved proverb status almost immediately.

The Spanish already had their own version:

> **'Absence leads to forgetting.'**

So did the French:

> **'Far from the eyes … far from the heart.'**

'Words are not birds
– once flown they can
never be caught.'
(Russia)

In 1929, American songwriters Joe Young and Sam Lewis identified the unspoken danger within Sextus Aurelius's original, and created a song with a cynical but possibly realistic title:

> **'Absence makes the heart grow fonder**
> **... for somebody else.'**

The bright young things of the social set had yet another version:

> **'Absinthe makes the heart grow fonder.'**

'Win a bet from your friend
and drink it on the spot.'
(Portugal)

Marriage

It is said that in courtship a man pursues a woman until she catches him. But is there a right speed?

'Marry in haste, repent at leisure.'

Some who are impatient are fortunate:

'Happy is the wooing that's not long in doing.'

Thomas Nashe in *Works* (1589) believed:

'He that marries late marries ill.'

But in his *Compleat Collection of English Proverbs* (1670), John Ray disagreed:

'It's good to marry late or never.'

'A fool goes to the sea but cannot find water there.'
(Iran)

It's hard to believe that

> **'Rain after the wedding is a sign of
> a fruitful marriage.'**

One wonders how marriages turn out in the Sahara, Sudan, Dubai, Arizona, the Gobi desert and Atacama in South America.

Why do the Scots dislike green?

> **'They that marry in green, their sorrow
> is soon seen.'**

Benjamin Franklin advised that

> **'If you want a neat wife, choose one
> on a Saturday.'**

Apart from the absurdity of this statement, Benjamin Franklin was in no position to give any guidance, as his own marriage was of doubtful legality and ultimately resulted in a ten-year separation.

> **'Beware of laughing hosts
> and weeping priests.'**
> (Germany)

In 1567 William Painter's *Palace of Pleasure* introduced into English:

> 'Marriages be don in heauen and performed in earth.'

which became:

> 'Marriages are made in heaven ...'

But did heaven make the divorce rate as well?

First heard in 1607 is this mixed blessing:

> 'Happy is the bride the sun shines upon, and happy is the corpse the rain rains on.'

While the Chinese predict:

> 'Dream of a funeral and you'll hear of a marriage.'

A Hebrew proverb advises:

> 'Adultery brings an early old age.'

A cautious piece of Scottish wisdom:

> 'Never marry for money – you can borrow it more cheaply.'

'Birds do not fly into our mouths ready roasted.'
(Italy)

Oddities

'A deaf husband and a blind wife
are always a happy couple.'

'Idleness is the ruin of chastity.'

'A man is a lion when single,
a peacock when engaged and
a beast of burden when married.'

The Spanish say:

> 'Choose neither a bride nor linens by the light of candles.'

And pragmatic Punjabis find comfort in:

> 'A fat spouse is a quilt for the winter.'

Finally, Jonathan Swift mentioned in *Polite Conversations* (1814) this bizarre belief:

> 'If you carry a nutmeg in your pocket you will marry an old man.'

> 'He who throws himself under the bench will be left to lie there.'
> (Denmark)

Take your pick

'Look before you leap'

or

'He who hesitates is lost.'

'Do not pay more for the
lining than for the cloth.'

(Turkey)

The Home

'Be it ever so humble,
there's no place like home.'

(John Howard Payne, 1823)

The Bible says:

'Ye shall kindle no fire throughout your
habitations upon the Sabbath day.'

(Exodus 35:3)

This might be a reasonable decree in the warm country
from which it arose, but it is questionable whether the
instruction is advisable, and it may even be unsafe in a
really cold country.

'He puts cheese in a
bottle then rubs bread
on the outside.'

(Iran)

A tidy house?

**'An apple, an egg and a nut,
you may eat after a slut.'**

Here 'slut' means a slovenly housewife, so if you are nervous about eating food from her dodgy kitchen, then an apple, an egg and a nut are okay, because their goodness is locked inside, impervious to dirt, and the external casing can be removed to eat what lies within.

**'Little birds may
peck a dead lion.'**
(Spain)

Invitations to clutter:

> **'Keep a thing for seven years and you'll always find a use for it.'**

And the open-ended:

> **'Lay things by – they may come to use.'**

If only. Many of us would do well to avoid this advice.

In 1799 Scottish poet Thomas Campbell penned the expression:

> **'Distance lends enchantment.'**

So the land agent hopes – but move closer and you might see the sewer pipes, the slag heaps, the neighbour's trampoline, the outdoor barbecue camping area and the sign saying 'Beach Too Dangerous For Swimming'.

'One cannot draw blood from a turnip, or ask a goat for wool.'
(Ireland)

An idea began with Cicero c.55 BC:

'What is more sacred, what more strongly guarded by every holy feeling, than a man's own home?'

By 1630 the notion had come into English, highlighted by Sir Edward Coke:

'A man's home is his castle.'

In the American Senate in 1880, Senator John J. Ingalls declared: 'Some orator said that though the winds of heaven might whistle around an Englishman's cottage, the King of England could not.' But in more recent times, in terms of privacy, this belief is under siege. Official social services, drug and crime detection, internet broadband, computer hacking, Wikileaks, line taps, telephoto lenses and sales-pitch 'cold calls' (especially by pre-recorded voices on computer-dialling) can all create a highway right into someone's privacy, often without their being able to stop it.

'The water is the same on both sides of the boat.'
(Finland)

And the family:

In c.1450 the publication of *Mirk's Festial* put into print the well-known homily of the time:

> **'Hyt ys old Englysch sawe: A mayde
> schuld be seen, but not herd.'**

This developed into:

> **'Children should be seen and
> not heard.'**

Maybe once upon a time. But the Duke of Windsor made a rather different discovery when he visited the US. 'The thing that impresses me the most about America,' he said, 'is the way parents obey their children.' (*Look*, 5 March 1957)

'If your enemy is an ant,
regard him as an elephant.'
(Turkey)

131

Oddities

Cervantes' character Don Quixote made the
first known reference to what became in English:

'It will all come out in the wash.'

Metaphorically, this has a certain credibility. But
in literal terms it is far from true – ask anyone
who has attempted to deal with stains from
beetroot, lily stamens or red wine. Perhaps
Cervantes didn't have to cope with such trivia.

Do we believe writers of commercial slogans?

**'The family that prays together
stays together.'**

This was written in 1942 by an advertising commercial
writer, Al Scalpone, to attract people to a Roman
Catholic 'Rosary' crusade.

And from around the world:

'A wee house has a wide throat.'

(Scotland)

'Better inside a cottage than
outside a castle.'

(Wales)

'When the next house is on fire
it is time to look to your own.'

(Nigeria)

'A small kitchen does not suffice
for two gluttons.'

(Italy)

'If you stay at home you won't
wear out your shoes.'

(Yiddish)

'Burn not your house to kill
the mice.'

(England)

Take your pick

'Money talks'

or

'Talk is cheap.'

'Don't bite until you
know if it is bread or a stone.'

(Italy)

Employment

'Working nine to five – what a way
to make a living.'

(Dolly Parton)

The New Testament advises:

'The labourer is worthy of his reward.'

(1 Timothy 5: 18)

But it is likely to be a CEO or a union that decides what the rate of the reward will be.

Equally fragile is:

'Jack is as good as his master.'

Some might have believed this in the days before Human Resources Administrators.

'Your belly is not filled by
your painting pictures of bread.'

(China)

'A new broom sweeps clean.'

In an employment situation, this often means that the 'new broom' will fire most of the long-serving employees.

The New Testament observes:

'Let every man abide in the same calling wherein he was called.'

(1 Corinthians 7:20)

Or in simple terms:

'Every man to his trade.'

But more recently opportunities have flourished so that people can 'expand professional horizons' with night school, extra-mural university courses – even internet tutoring.

'A blind man will not thank you for a looking glass.'

(England)

How seriously is this next advice taken?

'Experience is the best teacher.'

The adage is regarded with cynicism by anyone over 45 who applies for a job in which they've had 25 years of experience ... especially when a 23-year-old with an MBA applies for the same job.

In 1908 Swiss hotel proprietor César Ritz initiated the basis for what became a famous proverb:

'The customer is always right.'

This may be correct on the odd occasion. The other 99 percent of the time it is very unlikely.

**'No one with a good
catch of fish goes home
by the back alley.'**
(France)

Take your pick

'The only thing constant
is change'

or

'The more things change
the more they stay the same.'

'He who has good legs
often has bad boots.'

[Germany]

The Law

'The law is a ass – a idiot.'

(Mr Bumble in *Oliver Twist*)

Belief in a traditional piece of 'wisdom' can sometimes be of doubtful value:

'Possession is nine points of the law.'

Apparently back in 1595 this had some credence in law, but not any more. Show your stolen goods or put your tent up on someone else's front yard, and see what happens.

'Teeth put before the tongue give good advice.'
(Italy)

Also beware of:

'Imitation is the sincerest form of flattery.'

If imitation should slide into plagiarism or breach of copyright, then 'flattery' will take you right into court and a hefty fine.

Similarly:

**'Sticks and stones may break my bones
but words will never hurt me.'**

But just in case they do, a lawyer may be able to achieve some comforting damages under the various labels of libel, defamation, offensive words or 'language calculated to bring into disrepute'.

**'God gave us teeth to
hold back our tongue.'**
(Greece)

Here is another minefield:

'God helps those who help themselves.'

This really needs re-wording. Zenobius, a Greek teacher of rhetoric, originated this concept c. AD 120, and eventually it appeared in English (c.1580) as:

'God helps those who are industrious.'

Later it developed into:

**'Begin to help thyself and God will
help thee.'**

The later development into 'help yourself' has created a rather ambiguous concept. Being industrious is good, but 'help yourself' carries a connotation of uplifting things without permission or invitation – which isn't what was intended and can only lead to trouble.

'If it can lick, it can bite.'
(France)

From the 'Unwise to believe' department:

'Rules are made to be broken.'

This sounds light-hearted and gallant, but should be treated with supreme caution.

And what about:

'There is honour among thieves.'

Oh really?

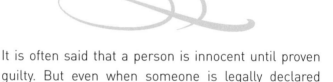

It is often said that a person is innocent until proven guilty. But even when someone is legally declared innocent, folklore sometimes ignores the real law:

**'Lizzie Borden took an axe,
And gave her mother forty whacks.
When she saw what she had done,
She gave her father forty-one.'**

After the axe murders occurred in 1893, Lizzie was tried, declared innocent and acquitted. But the facts were overlooked and the poem has kept going for over a century.

'If you have two loaves of bread, sell one and buy a lily.'
(China)

Many nations have a version of this proverb:

'Every land has its own law.'

Since every nation does indeed have its own law, this is completely valid. But the invention and rapid growth of internet usage has disestablished physical borders and thus created an entirely new lawlessness much more difficult to control.

In 43 BC Cicero mentioned:

'Things ill gotten slip away in evil ways.'

Progress into English came slowly, and by 1577 preacher John Northbrooke is attributed with the version:

'Euill gotten goods shall neuer prosper.'

Which became:

'Ill gotten goods never thrive.'

But historical analysis seems to provide evidence to the contrary, if the maxim is applied to 'colonising powers'

**'When bulls fight,
woe to the frogs.'**
(Portugal)

attaining territories by sometimes highly doubtful means. In post-colonial times, some of those colonies – India, New Zealand, the US, Australia, South Africa – seem to be doing all right.

Germany provides a pragmatic view:

> 'As fast as laws are devised, their evasion is contrived.'

While the Spanish quite cynically observe:

> 'Laws, like spider webs, catch flies, but let the hawk go free.'

A Russian proverb is even more cynical:

> 'God wanted to chastise mankind, so He sent lawyers.'

While the Japanese believe:

> 'Only lawyers and painters can turn white to black.'

But the Irish view could prove to be the most sensible:

> 'It is better to live unknown to the law.'

> 'He that is won with a nut may be lost with an apple.'
> (Romania)

Democracy

Since time immemorial, there has been an alarming number of pronouncements bad-mouthing democracy – not balanced by many proverbs in support.

A sentiment from ancient Rome was forthright:

> **'Nothing is so valueless as the sentiments of the mob.'**

Since then, others have been equally contemptuous of the value of public opinion. Philosophising British vicar Thomas Draxe, in his *Treasurie of Ancient Adagies* (1633), believed:

> **'He that builds on the people builds on the dirt.'**

'He who burns his buttocks must sit on blisters.'
(Holland)

Alexander Pope's *Imitations of Horace* in 1738 scorned the populace:

> 'The people are a many-headed beast.'

German philosopher Georg Wilhelm Hegel in 1821 believed:

> 'The people are that part of the state
> which does not know what it wants.'

Dr Vicesimus Knox in 1824 published an equally severe view:

> 'He who serves the public hath but
> a scurvy master.'

In his letter to Thomas Sterling in 1837, Thomas Carlyle wrote:

> 'The public is an old woman, let her
> maunder and mumble.'

While a German adage states:

> 'He who trusts the people hangs from a tree.'

'When a lion is old
he becomes a
plaything of jackals.'

(Iran)

American General William Tecumseh Sherman in 1863 was equally pessimistic:

> 'The voice of the people is the voice of humbug.'

And the following year British author John Ruskin quoted a 'Dr Chalmers' who believed:

> 'The public is just a great baby.'

Most crushing of all was a letter from the ecclesiastical scholar Alcuin of York to the King-Emperor Charlemagne in 798, debunking a line already in use, but which he recommended should not be observed:

> 'Nec audiendi qui solent dicere, vox populi, vox Dei, quum tumultuositas vulgi semper insaniae proxima sit.'

In other words:

> 'And those people should not be listened to

'Call me not olive
before you see me gathered.'
(Italy)

who say the voice of the people is the voice of God – the riotousness of the crowd is always very close to madness.'

Not everyone agreed. In Thomas Wright's 1839 collection of medieval protest songs, *Political Poems*, is the following wisdom from 1450, which keeps the essence but without the criticism:

'Peples vois is goddes voys ... men seyne.'

Eventually the nay-sayers were excluded and the maxim became:

'The voice of the people is the voice of God.'

But a character in George Bernard Shaw's 1903 play *Man and Superman* somewhat cryptically remarks:

'Democracy substitutes election by the incompetent many for appointment by the corrupt few.'

He later softened the remark slightly:

'Democracy is a device that insures we shall be governed no better than we deserve.'

'If you deal in camels, make the doors high.'
(Afghanistan)

Some balance had started by 1850 when Theodore Parker, a Christian minister in the US, pre-empted Lincoln by proclaiming:

> 'A government of all the people,
> by all the people, for all the people.'

Then along came Lord Bertrand Russell with:

> 'Democracy is the process by which
> people choose the man who'll get
> the blame.'

'The heaviest ear of corn
is the one with head bent low.'
(Ireland)

'The meek shall inherit the earth.'

This doesn't seem to apply to nations such as Japan and Germany, which have waged war, lost, then prospered.

Which all just goes to prove that the well-known philosopher Anon was correct in analysing that:

**'The world is divided into people
who think they are right.'**

'A man with a sour face
should not open a shop.'
(Japan)

Money

'Money governs the world.'

(Andreas Berthelson, *Dictionary*, 1754)

Later this became:

'Money makes the world go around
… that clinking clanking sound.'

(Fred Ebb, 1966)

'It is not the fault of
the post that the blind
man did not see it.'
(Sanskrit)

The New Testament tells us:

'The love of money is the root of all evil.'

(1 Timothy 6: 10)

And the Gospels advise:

'It is easier for a camel to go through the eye of a needle than for a rich person to enter the Kingdom of God.'

(Luke 18: 25)

But we are also told in the Bible:

'Wealth makes friends.'

(Proverbs 19: 4)

Which somehow carries an ironic implication that those who cultivate the friendship of the rich are not interested in friendships with the poor.

'If the camel but gets its nose in a tent, the body will soon follow.'

(Arabia)

Writers of wisdom have many different takes on the subject:

> 'A heavy purse makes a light heart.'

> 'Money is a fruit that is always ripe.'

> 'Money is only good for weekdays, holidays and rainy days.'

> 'What words won't do, gold will.'

> 'A man without money is a bow without an arrow.'

> 'Money has no smell.'

> 'Wealth is wisdom – he that is rich is wise.'

Not everyone agreed. In 322 BC, Aristotle offered a low opinion of the gilded classes:

> 'The character which results from wealth is that of a prosperous fool.'

In 1598, Ben Jonson in his play *The Case is Altered* referred to 'an old proverb':

> 'Gold is but muck.'

> 'The best advice is found on the pillow.'
> (Denmark)

Paroemiologia Anglo-Latina (1639) decreed that 'it is better to have good fortune than be a rich man's child', which over centuries modified into:

'Better to be born lucky than rich.'

In 1640, Welsh poet George Herbert in *Jacula Prudentum* somewhat cryptically opined that:

'Health without wealth is half a sickness.'

And in 1659, British historian James Howell decided that:

'A man's wealth is his enemy.'

The Spanish have a cynical assessment:

'A rich man is either a scoundrel or the heir of one.'

'After shaving there is nothing to shear.'

(France)

Francis Bacon elaborated on Ben Jonson's belief that 'Gold is but muck' in his *Essay 85* (1625):

> **'Money is like muck – not good unless it be spread.'**

A further reincarnation appeared in Thornton Wilder's 1958 play *The Matchmaker*:

> **'Money is like manure; it's not worth a thing unless it's spread around.'**

The thought became even more famous in the musical adaptation, *Hello Dolly!*

'A bird may be very small but always seeks a nest of its own.'
(Denmark)

155

Now here is an odd juxtaposition:

> **'Cheese and money should always
> sleep together one night.'**

This is believed to mean that money should be paid in advance of goods being uplifted.

Wasteful living has been described as:

> **'To bring ninepence to nothing.'**

In other words, neglect your property or inheritance and it will dwindle away.

Similarly:

> **'He hath whittled a mill-post to
> a pudding-prick.'**

Again this indicates that a fortune has been spent and dissipated through over-indulgence and unwise living. (A pudding-prick is an unfortunate early name for a kitchen skewer.)

**'A bowl should not laugh
when a calabash breaks.'**
(West Africa)

An English proverb from the 17th century presents an intriguing image:

'It is hard to pull a stocking off a bare leg.'

Which means that the money has run out and no more is available.

A Greek image has a similar significance:

**'A thousand men cannot undress
a naked man.'**

'Advice is cheap.'

This is not always true. Should you seek the guidance of a financial consultant, medical specialist, dietician, life coach, careers adviser, spiritualist, palm reader or colour co-ordinator, you'll pay.

**'It is pleasant to
command, even if
only a herd of cattle.'**
(Spain)

In 1870, supreme salesman P.T. Barnum offered these cautionary words:

'When people expect to get "something for nothing" they are sure to be cheated.'

But in 1927 an American song with words by Lew Brown and Buddy DeSylva became famous with its expression of optimism:

'The best things in life are free.'

This depends on what you consider to be 'the best things'. The moon, the stars, the flowers in spring and robins that sing are all free, but most other things aren't.

An old proverb which sounds like a modern credit card advertisement, actually surfaced in England as far back as 1546:

'Spend – and God will send.'

'When cat and mouse
agree, the farmer
has no chance.'
(Denmark)

But not everyone encouraged reckless spending. In 1639 an alternative version emerged in Britain:

'He that has lost his credit is dead to the world.'

And an Italian saying has it that:

'Credit lost is like a broken mirror.'

However, in more recent times American Express, Visa and MasterCard will happily rush in where a bank might fear to tread.

Thomas Tusser urged caution in his *Five Hundred Pointes of Good Husbandrie* (1573):

'A foole & his money, be soone at debate.'

Which a few years later had smoothed into:

'A fool and his money are soon parted.'

Even before Shakespeare mentioned it (in *Hamlet*), there was a proverb that said:

'Lend your money and lose your friend.'

'An aged willow is difficult to bend.'
(Ireland)

And Greek wisdom agrees:

> **'Eat and drink with your relatives,
> do business with strangers.'**

The Spaniards have a saying:

> **'A dollar today is worth more than
> a dollar tomorrow.'**

Therefore gather ye a mortgage while ye may.

Italians have advanced cynicism about government cash resources:

> **'Public money is like holy water –
> everyone helps himself to it.'**

> **'Beautiful flowers fade,
> but weeds last right
> through the season.'**
> (Sweden)

Take your pick

'The art of getting rich
consists very much in thrift'

(Benjamin Franklin)

or

'Thrift makes one a slave.'

(Burma)

'The peony is beautiful
but it must be supported
by green leaves.'

(China)

Oddities

'A rich man and a spittoon get dirtier
as they accumulate.'

(Japan)

'Money can buy you a fine dog,
but only love can make it wag its tail.'

(Spain)

'Gold opens every door save Heaven's.'

(Germany)

'No man is so rich as to say "I have enough".'

(Ancient Rome)

'A glimpse of money makes even
the blind man see.'

(China)

'Add up your pennies and buy a hen.'

(Poland)

'Real wealth consists not in having,
but in not wanting.'

(Italy)

'It is not the man who has too little,
but the man who craves more
who is poor.'

(Ireland)

'Getting money is like digging with
a needle; spending it is like water
soaking into sand.'

(Japan)

Investment

In 1732 Thomas Fuller printed the following investment advice:

> **'If thou wouldst keep money, save money,**
> **If thou wouldst reap money, sow money.'**

Another version already existed. Thomas Wilson's *Discourse on Usury* (1572) decreed:

> **'Money begets money.'**

As did the advice:

> **'Nothing venture, nothing have.'**

From France came:

> **'To a bold man fortune holds out her hand.'**

'Anger is a stone cast
into a wasps' nest.'

(India)

Not forgetting:

'If you don't speculate you can't accumulate.'

In 1931 Henry Ford weighed in with:

**'Money is like an arm and a leg –
use it or lose it.'**

On the other hand, Fannie Mae, Enron and Bernie Madoff might have been restrained had they followed Lord Berners' more cautious wisdom in *Huon de Bordeaux* (1534):

'He that ventures too far loses all.'

This was echoed in Richard Tarlton's *Newes out of Purgatory* (1590):

'Men that venture little, hazard little.'

Total caution was advocated by Polonius in Shakespeare's *Hamlet*:

'Neither a borrower nor a lender be.'

**'No ape but swears he
has the handsomest children.'**
(Germany)

The most cautious of all – and likely to be the oldest opinion on the matter – can be traced back to Aesop in 500 BC. Its first appearance in English was in 1470:

> **'Betyr ys a byrd in the hond than tweye in the wode.'**

Otherwise known as:

> **'A bird in the hand is worth two in the bush.'**

> **'As you sow so shall you reap.'**

This advice can be unreliable. Not everyone accepts the consequences of their actions. For example, dishonest financiers who have radiated integrity but actually created disaster tend to remain in their mansions without a backward glance at what they have sown: the ruin of helpless investors who are crippled by bankruptcy and forced to sell their homes.

> **'It is a small honour for the lion who seizes a mouse.'**
> (Germany)

Oddities

'A dealer in rubbish
sings the praise of rubbish.'

(Italy)

'It is a bad hen which eats at your house
and lays at another's.'

(Spain)

'Always bargain on a full stomach.'

(Korea)

'Hunger is a poor adviser.'

(Mexico)

'Eat vegetables and fear no creditor,
rather than eat roast duck and hide.'

(Yiddish)

Take your pick

From Denmark:

**'Fortune often knocks at the door,
but the fool does not invite her in.'**

A Yiddish proverb:

'When Fortune calls, offer her a chair.'

Or this German opinion:

**'What fortune gives today,
it takes away tomorrow.'**

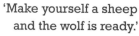

'Make yourself a sheep
and the wolf is ready.'

(Iran)

Poverty

**'The poor you will always
have with you.'**

(Matthew 26: 11)

or

**'He who mocks the poor shows
contempt for their maker.'**

(Proverbs 17: 5)

American actress Mae West had natural pulchritude, salty wit and a joyous celebration of physical relationships (she once said 'I've been in more laps than a napkin'). But she retained a cautious eye on staying rich enough to be comfortable. Her theory:

**'Love conquers all things except
poverty and toothache.'**

'Never write a letter
when you are angry.'
(China)

A Hebrew version takes an alternative view:

> 'A woman prefers poverty with love
> to wealth without love.'

The French were a little more optimistic, as reflected in Geoffrey Chaucer's translation of *The Romance of the Rose* (c.1370):

> 'For, whan Richesse shyneth bright,
> Love recovereth ageyn his light;
> And whan it faileth, he wol flit.
> And as she groweth, so groweth it.'

This at least allowed that love could be regained – when the coffers began to fill.

English poet Richard Braithwaite was less sanguine. His treatise called *The English Gentlewoman* (1631) puts it on the line:

> 'It hath been an old maxime – that as
> poverty goes in at one doore, love goes
> out at the other.'

From Africa comes:

> 'You cannot amuse a hungry person.'

'Don't look for apples
under a poplar tree.'
(Slavic)

A gently optimistic thought from Greece:

> '**Painless poverty is better than
> embittered wealth.**'

And a Chinese proverb celebrates loyalty in spite of
all:

> '**A dog won't forsake its master
> because of poverty.**'

'**Dry reeds do not seek
the company of fire.**'
(Arabia)

Take your pick

St Matthew encourages us to

'Seek and ye shall find'

[Matthew 7: 7]

but British playwright Ben Jonson in 1598
launched the caution which later became

'Curiosity killed the cat.'

'Never argue with a man
who buys ink by the barrel.'

(China)

Animals

There are hundreds of proverbs which use animals as a metaphor for human behaviour. Some are clever:

'The calf, the goose and the bee – the world is ruled by just these three.'

In other words, parchment, wax and pen – i.e. documentation – 'rule the world'.

'Fish swim three times.'

The three times are first in water, then in batter and finally in hot oil!

Others are not so clever:

'He that will meddle with all things may go shoe the goslings.' (1434)

Now what can that mean?

'Trust in God but tie
up your camel.'
(Iran)

'Agues come on horseback, but go away on foot.'

In other words, fevers strike quickly but are slow to heal.

'Because a man is born in a stable, that does not make him a horse.'

Attributed to the first Duke of Wellington, after he got fed up with being teased about being Irish-born.

'To have a colt's tooth ...'

This dates from 1368 and indicates that although someone might be getting on in years, their energy and mental attitude remain youthful.

'Money makes the mare to go.'

If 'to go' is shorthand for 'go fast', then the image holds no particular proof that mares will win heavily-bet races.

'Lend thy horse for a long journey – thou mayst have him again with his skin.'

This was published in 1659 by James Howell. Perhaps it means that whoever borrowed the horse will ride it to a frazzle!

'Even should the snake be small, it is wise to hit it with a big stick.'
(India)

'Rein in the horse at the edge of the cliff.'

You'd be silly not to.

In 1831 Benjamin Disraeli gave us the term:

'A dark horse.'

Originally it referred to a little-noticed horse which unexpectedly wins a race. It was later applied to any successful human equivalent.

'Horse feathers.'

Because horses don't have feathers, this is a put-down designating a previous statement as false, nonsense, lies.

'If two ride on a horse, one must ride behind.'

There can't be two leaders or two bosses.

'Arrogance is a weed which grows mainly on a dunghill.'
(Arabia)

> '**Where the deer is slain, there will some of his blood lie.**'

This is only to be expected – but in 1732 it was regarded as a piece of wisdom.

Horses for courses:

> '**A short horse is soon curried.**'
> (Spain)

> '**You cannot shoe a running horse.**'
> (Holland)

> '**The master's eye is the best curry comb.**'
> (Ireland)

> '**A man on horseback doesn't recognise his father.**'
> (Russia)

> '**Straight from the horse's mouth.**'
> (P.G. Wodehouse, 1928)

'**To have a calf, ask for an ox.**'
(Germany)

'The calf never heard a church bell.'

Apparently this refers to an animal born and then killed between two Sundays.

'To eat the calf in the cow's belly.'

This refers to unwisely counting on the profit to be made from pregnant cattle whose calves will be sold when born – if all goes well. It is the bovine version of counting your chickens before they are hatched.

'When the ox falls there are many that will kill him.'

A belief, attributed to the Dutch, that when a flaw is revealed in an important person, attacks on their standing and reputation will start.

'The boy has gone by with the cows.'

In Oxford folklore, this refers to someone who has missed a good opportunity.

'Measure forty times before cutting once.'
(Turkey)

'He has an ill look among lambs.'

This is believed to refer to someone whose appearance and demeanour gives the impression of being untrustworthy.

'Much cry and little wool.'

Originally 'Moche crye and no wull', this means that someone is showy but lacks substance – an 18th century equivalent of 'Big hat and no cattle', 'All coffee and no omelette' or 'Many frills but no knickers'.

'One sheep follows another.'

Sir Walter Scott felt moved to introduce this in *Old Mortality* (1816) as a piece of wisdom, though most folk knew it already.

And don't forget:

'It is idle to swallow the cow and choke on the tail'

and

'A bad ploughman quarrels with his ox.'
(Korea)

'When I put my hand to my head I find there is no hat.'
(Iran)

'Beware of the octopus's eighth leg.'

Quirky though it sounds, this curiosity from Samoa has validity within the right context. You might think everything in a project is organised, but if you take your eye off one detail for a moment, it might all go askew. It's a Polynesian equivalent of Murphy's Law.

A porcine selection:

'A pig bought on credit is forever grunting.'

'It's the quiet pigs who eat the grain.'

'Don't give cherries to pigs or advice to fools.'

'A pig's tail will never make a good arrow.'

'Safe as a sow in a gutter.'

'Old habits are shirts made of iron.'
(Slavic)

'There is more than one way to skin a cat.'

Some claim that this refers to skinning catfish rather than actual cats. When it comes to skinning actual cats ... well, there is only one way.

'Turn the cat in the pan.'

This emerged in 1384 to describe someone imparting news, gossip or their opinion to another person – but pretending they were reporting what someone else had said. This shows that as far back as the 1300s someone in the news had 'a friend' or 'a reliable source' who was willing to be quoted. (It isn't clear what a cat in a pan had to do with it.)

'Long and slender like a cat's elbow.'

This may surprise anyone who has never thought about cats having an elbow, but the image of slim lean elegance does have some validity.

'Send not a cat for lard.'

Why would you?

'A cat dreams all night of a sheep's tail.'

Maybe so – but how does anyone really know?

'An ass's tail will not make a good sieve.'

(Italy)

'Cats have nine lives.'

Of course they don't. Like all living creatures, cats have only one life. But their extraordinary agility in escaping danger is often demonstrated, which led the ancient Egyptians (who worshipped cats as gods anyway) to believe the creatures had a godlike quality of multiple lives. The Egyptians settled on nine because they regarded three as a 'significant' number, and three times three was a highly honoured combination. Hence they said of the moggy that it lived eight more lives than mere humans. Several thousand years later we're still saying it.

'Throw him into a
river and he will rise
with a fish in his mouth.'
(Arabia)

'As busy as a dog in dough.'

An old Shropshire saying which is fun but surely imaginary, since the reality cannot have been observed very often.

'He is a good dog which goes to church.'

Sir Walter Scott referred to this in 1836 as 'an old proverb', based on a respected nobleman's mastiff which accompanied him to church with dignity, only occasionally howling when the hymns were sung. Over time, the image of the well-behaved dog came to refer to people who could adjust their behaviour and demeanour to fit neatly into any circumstance.

'Love will make a dog howl in rhyme.'

An image introduced by dramatists Francis Beaumont and John Fletcher (c. 1600) in *Queen of Corinth*, but one suspects the howling dog would be motivated by lust rather then love.

'Fleas jump on a sickly dog.'

Misfortunes crowd one on top of another.

'If you want an audience,
start a fight.'
(China)

'It would vex a dog to see a pudding creep.'

The meaning is a mystery.

Horace declaimed in the *Satires*:

'Hungry dogs will eat dirty puddings.'

Didn't he know that hungry dogs will eat almost any-thing dirty?

Some canine saws to reflect on:

'Would you live long – be healthy not fat,
drink like a dog and eat like a cat.'

'Dogs bark but the caravan goes on.'

'A dog with a bone knows no friends.'

'The moon does not heed the barking
of dogs.'

'Hunger is a good
kitchen to a cold potato.'
(Japan)

'Don't pour water on a drowned mouse.'

This is related to such sayings as 'Don't mock the afflicted' or 'Don't kick a man when he is down', except that the mouse in the original is already dead.

'A mouse must not think to cast a shadow like an elephant.'

'A dead mouse feels no cold.'

'It is indiscreet for a rat to gnaw at a tiger's tail.'

(China)

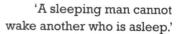

'A sleeping man cannot wake another who is asleep.'

(Hindu)

All birds together …

'There's many a good cockerel comes
out of a tattered bag.'

'The owl always believes his own son
is a hawk.'

'A wet bird never flies at night.'

'A black hen can lay a white egg.'

'Out of a white egg often comes a black chick.'

'A wise falcon hides its talons.'
(Denmark)

'A blind hen can sometimes find corn.'
(France)

'A bird chooses a sturdy branch before
alighting.'
(Korea)

'The bird hunting the locust is unaware
of the hawk hunting him.'
(Portugal)

'Don't use an axe
to embroider.'
(Malaysia)

'To chance the ducks.'

Although ducks would seem to be fairly low on the scale of risky behaviour, the saying refers to a person who goes ahead with a plan regardless of what the possible outcome or effects might be.

Or does it mean those rows of ducks you can 'shoot' at a fairground?

'Duck soup.'

Describes something which can be done easily. Nobody knows why it means that – even the Marx Brothers didn't know.

'Drunk as an owl.' ('Boiled as an owl.')

Owls, although never actually drunk, were often associated with foolish behaviour, and their round-eyed gaze sometimes resembled the vacant stare of a drunkard. 'Boiled' is an old synonym for drunk.

'Given the bird.'

To be dismissed – often heard in show business to describe a performer being booed or ridiculed. The reference is based on the sound of geese hissing.

'If a donkey goes travelling he will not come home a horse.'

(France)

'If it walks like a duck, quacks like a duck, and looks like a duck, it must be a duck.'

When evidence is overwhelming, assume that the obvious is true.

'He that would have eggs must endure the cackling of hens.'

You must be willing to endure unpleasant, irritating things in order to get what you want.

'Birds of a feather flock together.'

Yes they do, but sometimes only temporarily if they are Members of Parliament or delegates at major APEC or EU meetings – and whether or not the flocking together actually achieves anything is open to question. Some family reunions can also be deceptive: for some individuals there is often a strong desire to flock somewhere else.

'Avoid a strange dog, a flood, and a man who thinks he is wise.'
(Wales)

Fishy business ...

'You must lose a fly to catch a trout.'

'There is no eel so small but it hopes to become a whale.'

'Mud chokes no eels.'

'A frog does not jump in the daytime without reason.'
(Nigeria)

'In still waters are the largest fish.'

'Of all God's creatures the salmon is the cleanest.'
(Wales)

'The frog in the well knows nothing of the ocean.'
(Japan)

'He who sleeps catches no fish.'

'Where there are no swamps there are no frogs.'

'A carpenter may lend his wife but not his tools.'
(Korea)

'If frogs had wheels, they wouldn't bump their backsides.'

It is useless to wish for impossible things.

'Happy as a clam.'

The full proverb is 'Happy as a clam at high tide', because that is when the clam is safest.

'The world's mine oyster.'

From Shakespeare's *The Merry Wives of Windsor* (1600), this means anything is available to you.

'The shell of a clam is free from rust.'

(Korea)

'Only a lame crab walks straight.'

(Afghanistan)

'Fear not the wind if your haystacks are tied down.'

(Ireland)

'Where bees are, there is honey.'

'Insects do not nest in a busy door-hinge.'
(China)

'Better to be an ant's head than a
lion's tail.'
(Armenia)

'A dead bee maketh no honey.'
(1572)

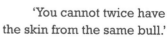

'You cannot twice have
the skin from the same bull.'
(Russia)

'A sly rabbit will have three openings
to his den.'

(China)

'Do not speak ill of a rhinoceros if there
is no tree nearby.'

(Zululand)

'A tortoise makes progress when it sticks
its neck out.'

(Spain)

'He who rides a tiger is afraid to dismount.'

(Japan)

'If you try to store milk
in a sieve, do not
complain of bad luck.'

(Afghanistan)

'Drunk as a skunk.'

Skunks are seldom if ever drunk. The use of rhyme and the lack of attraction associated with skunks give the proverb its cogency.

'The leopard does not change its spots.'

The leopard doesn't, but makeover consultants, hair stylists, modelling schools, fashion magazines and the entire self-improvement industry would go out of business if superficial 'spot-changing' were not possible.

'By candlelight a goat
looks like a lady.'
(France)

An observation from Jonathan Swift (1706) assuring us of something we'd probably never thought of:

'Elephants are always drawn smaller than life, but a flea always larger.'

'Mackerel sky and mares' tails make lofty ships carry low sails.'

Sailors do know this one. Mackerel skies and mares' tails describe two kinds of clouds – cirro-cumulus and twisted sheaves of cirrus respectively – implying strong high-level winds and possible rain.

'Warm up a frozen snake and she will bite you.'
(Armenia)

Oddities

'One man may steal a horse while another
may not look over a hedge.'

'He that makes his mistress a goldfinch
may make her a wagtail.'
(1647)

'Take your thanks to feed your cat.'
(Scotland)

'Fat as a hen in the forehead.'

'To smile like a brewer's horse.'

'A precipice in front of you,
wolves behind you – that is life.'
(Russia)

'Seldom dieth the ox that weepeth
for the cock.'

'The parrot must have an almond.'

'If thou hast not a capon,
feed on an onion.'
(France)

'If the cat were a hen it too would
lay eggs.'
(Germany)

'The butterfly often forgets it was
a caterpillar.'
(Sweden)

'It does not depend upon the dog
where the horse shall die.'
(Denmark)

'If you were born lucky
even your rooster will lay eggs.'
(Russia)

And a couplet worth pondering:

'When the rain raineth and
the goose winketh,
Little wots the gosling what
the goose thinketh.'

Take your pick

'You can't teach an old dog
new tricks'

or

'You are never too old
to learn.'

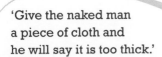

'Give the naked man
a piece of cloth and
he will say it is too thick.'
(Russia)

Books

'A house without books is like
a room without windows.'

(Heinrich Mann)

Back in 1597 Francis Bacon advised:

'Reading makes a full man.'

But early Americans were nervous that reading was too
solitary an occupation to be healthy, so opined that:

'Reading rots the brain.'

Dissension on the matter is widespread. Ralph Waldo
Emerson felt that

**'Some books leave us free and some
books make us free.'**

**'A bagpipe never utters
a word until its belly is full.'**

(France)

In Japan:

> 'Books are preserved minds.'

And two from China:

> 'A book holds a house of gold.'

> 'A book is like a garden carried in the pocket.'

But others are ambivalent. Do they mean 'yes' or 'no'?

From Welsh poet George Herbert (c.1630):

> 'Woe be to him that reads but one book.'

From Russia:

> 'Good scribes are not those who write well, but who erase well.'

This might mean 'Don't overwrite by using three words where one would do', or does it mean 'Erase the whole lot, we don't want it'?

> 'Go to law for a sheep and lose your cow.'
> (Greece)

From Belgium:

> **'The head is older than the book.'**

Mysterious. It might mean our heads know more than any printed page.

From Henry Wadsworth Longfellow:

> **'Books are sepulchres of thought.'**

A sepulchre is a burial vault, so did he mean that all books are 'dead' material?

From the Netherlands:

> **'Other people's books are difficult to read.'**

From China:

> **'One is happy when one has books, but happier still when one has no need of them.'**

Italy can be uncompromising:

> **'There is no worse robber than a bad book.'**

And Germany presents a bizarre image:

> **'It is not healthy to swallow books without chewing.'**

'The eagle flies in the sky but nests on the ground.'
(Albania)

Definitely not in favour are:

'Think much, say little, write less.'
(France)

'Where hands are needed, words and letters are useless.'
(Germany)

'Wise silence has never been written down.'
(Italy)

'We cannot learn men from books.'
(Benjamin Disraeli)

'Books are the blessed chloroform of the mind.'
(Robert W. Chambers)

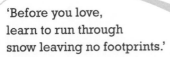

**'Before you love,
learn to run through
snow leaving no footprints.'**
(Turkey)

Dating from 1929, there is some truth in this American saying:

'Don't judge a book by its cover.'

We are taught not to take outward appearance too seriously, but in the real world the publishing industry does its best to counteract any such truth. Large sums are allocated to ensure that a book is adorned with a cover so attractive that the wallet is reached for while the cover is in sight ... and the proverb is out of mind.

'Even a clock which
does not work is
correct twice a day.'
(Poland)

Here is a proverb already considered old in 1750, when its full wording was:

> **'When house and land are gone and spent,**
> **then learning is most excellent.'**

Eventually it narrowed down to:

> **'Learning is better than house and land.'**

This seems supportable until examined more closely. Are we being asked to do without a roof over our heads in a cold climate, in favour of reading Carlyle or the Encyclopaedia Britannica? Or is the truth of the adage in recognising that there are people in old folks' homes who, though without their house and land, might still enjoy reading and even learning, and are therefore passing their time rather more usefully. If so, then one has an image of elderly folk in rest homes, bright-eyed and bushy-tailed, tackling university courses in classic literature and astrophysics. Yeah, right.

'Never marry a widow
unless her first husband
was hanged.'
(Scotland)

Oddities

'Scholars talk books;
butchers talk pigs.'

(China)

'When in anger,
say the alphabet.'

(USA)

'Those who can read and write
have four eyes.'

(Albania)

'The wise read a letter backwards.'

(Germany)

'Those who read many epitaphs
lose their memory.'

(Latin)

What is attractive about anything forbidden? An Italian proverb says:

> 'A book whose sale is forbidden …
>> all men rush to see,
> For prohibition turns …
>> one reader into three!'

Finally, with an echo of *Dead Poets Society*, a piece of Italian wisdom says:

> 'Poets and pigs are appreciated
> only after their death.'

'To be red-headed
is better then to be
without a head.'
(Ireland)

Take your pick

'Two heads are better than one'

or

'Paddle your own canoe.'

'Chickens are slow in
coming from unlaid eggs.'
(Germany)

Pictures

'What is the use of a book,'
thought Alice, 'without pictures
or conversations?'

(Lewis Carroll)

An old Latin adage says:

'Mutum est pictura poema.'
'A picture is a mute poem.'

But later, c. AD 400, St Augustine thundered:

'Pictures are the books of the ignorant.'

'Throwing pebbles at an
elephant does not disturb him.'
(Africa)

However, Russian novelist Ivan Turgenev, not usually considered ignorant, wrote in *Fathers and Sons* (1862):

'A picture shows me at a glance what it takes dozens of pages of a book to expound.'

A related but rephrased version of this appeared in 1911, and is attributed to American editor Arthur Brisbane:

'Use a picture – it's worth a thousand words.'

Within a few years this had smoothed into:

'A picture is worth a thousand words.'

Meanwhile, in 1906 a series of American advertisements appeared for kidney pills, showing someone in pain holding their back. The caption quickly became accepted wisdom:

'Every picture tells a story.'

By the middle of the 20th century, printed cartoon versions of famous stories, once known as 'classic comics', were restyled as 'graphic novels'.

St Augustine seems to have lost that one.

'You can't catch two frogs with one hand.'
(China)

Knowledge

'Real knowledge is to know
the extent of one's ignorance.'

(Confucius)

Sir Francis Bacon's *Religious Meditations* (1597) made
this concept famous:

'Knowledge is power.'

Alas, this rather conflicts with George Pettie's assertion
in 1576:

'So long as I know it not, it hurteth mee not.'

Later modified into:

'What you don't know can't hurt you.'

'Oil and truth will
get uppermost last.'
(Italy)

This is untrue in so many ways it would be difficult to enumerate them all: the beginnings of cancer; the vehicle about to speed through the intersection you are sedately driving towards; the hidden collapse of a financial investment; the thug hiding in the shadows with a mallet ...

Similarly it's necessary to be aware of the legal maxim:

'Ignorantia iuris neminem excusat.'

'Ignorance of the law excuses no one.'

Chopping down a suburban tree or lighting a backyard bonfire may be a serious breach of local law – and not knowing about it won't help if you are caught.

In 1861, Count Johann Bernhard said of a political decision:

'Not worth the paper it's written on.'

This may be an effective put-down in a specific political context, but is a bit risky is other circumstances. After all, nine publishers made a similar dismissal when they turned down the first *Harry Potter* manuscript.

'He is alive because he cannot afford a funeral.'
(Iran)

First noticed in an 1855 poem by Robert Browning and rapidly perceived as wisdom:

'Less is more.'

This is certainly admirable advice when applied to some situations, such as speeches or written accounts which go on far too long when a dozen words would have done. But its profundity is expressed so economically that at first it seems hard to fathom such an oxymoron. 'Fat is thin' doesn't quite work the same way.

'A dog does not resent being called a dog.'
(Africa)

'Practise what you preach.'

Does this mean Catholic priests and nuns must tell their congregations to be celibate?

'One half of the world doesn't know how the other half lives.'

Maybe this was so in earlier times. But with satellite television, Michael Palin, David Bellamy, BBC World Service, *National Geographic* magazine, Bear Grylls, Sir David Attenborough, the Sky Adventure channel and endless frenetic forays into international cooking, a good number of people now have a fair idea of how others live.

'A red chilli under deep water will still taste hot.'

(Burma)

'Every cloud has a silver lining.'

This is admirable optimism from the school of thought which says 'everything bad has something good about it' or 'it will all come right in the end'. But those who have been devastated by a flood, tornado, tsunami, drought, bushfire or earthquake might regard it with a more jaundiced eye.

Two proverbs from the Orient:

**'He who knows does not talk,
he who talks does not know.'**

(China)

**'Knowledge without wisdom is a load
of books on the back of an ass.'**

(Japan)

**'He that is bald has
no need for a comb.'**

(India)

'The more things change, the more they stay the same.'

It is hard to accept that things 'stay the same' when you consider that now phones can also tell the time, take photos and send written messages. And we're able to open the garage door without getting out of the car.

'Where ignorance is bliss, 'tis folly to be wise.'

This can be hard to justify. Try telling it to anyone who didn't notice they'd parked their car in a 24-hour tow-away zone.

'No fishes are required in a pond which has no water.'

(Iran)

News

'The news from Austria
are very sad.'

(Queen Victoria, 1861)

President Thomas Jefferson asserted rather cynically in 1820:

'Nothing can now be believed which
is seen in a newspaper.'

Nearly a century later, American observer, philosopher and writer Will Rogers didn't agree, and is attributed with:

'All I know is what I see in the papers.'

'Cows have no
business in horseplay.'
(Jamaica)

John Clarke confidently stated in his *Paroemiologia Anglo-Latina* (1639):

'Seeing is believing.'

But when it comes to photography, this may not always be true. Cameras and photographs first appeared during the mid 1800s. Soon after that, the expression 'The camera cannot lie' came into use, based on the belief that while paintings could 'enhance' a subject, cameras showed only the truth. The term's first known appearance in print was in a Nebraska newspaper in 1895, but even at that early stage there was a hint of irony in its use.

When American documentary-photographer Lewis Hine commented on the matter at the end of the century, the expression had been modified into 'The camera never lies' – to which Hine added: 'but liars may photograph'. And indeed they did.

'One man tells a lie –
dozens repeat it as the truth.'

(China)

'The camera never lies.'

To be fair, the camera itself usually doesn't lie, although as Lewis Hine said, it has been tricked. In 1917 two children, Elsie Wright and Frances Griffiths, produced photographs of 'fairies'. Sir Arthur Conan Doyle published the photos of the 'Cottingley Fairies' as proof that fairies existed, and for many years the world believed they were real. Then it was revealed they were really paper cut-outs attached to slim hat pins. Other deceptions are more obvious: for example, those cheerful tourists carefully placed with arm outstretched, appearing to 'push' the Leaning Tower of Pisa.

But inventions such as PhotoShop, PaintShop Pro and Computer Generated Imagery (CGI) can create far more convincing falsehoods by 'adjustments' either before or after the picture is actually taken. Some magazines employ 'illustration enhancers' whose job is to ensure that photographs evoke a blemish-free view of anyone and everything. Many images we now see cannot be believed.

'When the soup is boiling over, a ladle is not too costly.'
(Turkey)

The 'prophesies' of Old Mother Shipton (1488-1561) were first printed in 1641 – but later editors tinkered with, and added to, the originals so it was difficult to know which were the old lady's supposed predictions, and which weren't.

The publisher of the 1862 edition was forced to admit that he had invented some of the predictions he had claimed to discover in a book nearly two centuries old – they simply weren't Mother Shipton's at all.

But whether originating in 1641 or 1862, her predictions pre-dated television and Twitter – and this prophesy certainly came true:

**'Around the world thoughts shall fly,
in the twinkling of an eye.'**

**'The afternoon knows what
the morning never suspected.'**
(Sweden)

**'Laugh and the world laughs with you,
weep and you weep alone.'**

Not always true. If you weep and if you have any news value, you won't be alone for long. Cameras will rush to feature you on the front page and on the evening television news.

In 1477 William Caxton, full of good intentions, opined:

'Discretion is the better part of valour.'

Since then the tabloid press has become dedicated to dislodging discretion wherever possible, often by offering a handsome payment for all to be revealed.

'There will be trouble if the
cobbler starts making pies.'
(Russia)

Take your pick

'Do unto others as you would have
others do unto you'

or

'Nice guys finish last.'

'Who keeps company with
wolves will learn to howl.'

(Italy)

Friends, Neighbours, Visitors

'Travel along, singing a song,
side by side.'

(Harry Woods, 1927)

'United we stand – divided we fall.'

This thought has a pleasing affinity with:

'One good turn deserves another.'

But they sit uncomfortably next to:

'Every man for himself.'

'In a court of fowls, the
cockroach never wins a case.'

(Rwanda)

To say nothing of:

'It's a dog eat dog world.'

The image of ruthless competition and self-interest is harsh and effective and makes an impact – but it is based on falsehood. Dogs fight other dogs but don't eat them (because generally carnivores do not eat other carnivores).

In 1559 Thomas Becon's *Prayers* created a proverb whose immediate impact is now somewhat reduced:

'To agree like harp and harrow.'

The significance is that two objects – a harp and a harrow – are so vastly different that they could never be expected to agree (rather like chalk and cheese). Commentators believed that the harp and the harrow were thinly veiled references to God and the devil.

'Going to bed early
to save candles is false
economy if the result is twins.'
(China)

'Close neighbours are better than
distant relatives.'

(Japan)

The Old Testament advocates being a good neighbour:

'Thou shalt love thy neighbour as thyself.'

(Leviticus 19:18)

In 1640 Welsh poet George Herbert agreed, but with a
reservation:

'Love your neighbour – yet pull not downe
your hedge.'

A Yiddish proverb provides bonhomie with realism:

'Mix with the neighbours and you learn
what's doing in your own house.'

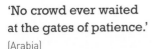

'No crowd ever waited
at the gates of patience.'

(Arabia)

The Chinese advise:

> **'Have but few friends though much acquaintance.'**

Even if you've never actually met any of them (i.e. on Twitter, Facebook, Myspace, etc.).

> **'Two's company, three's a crowd.'**

In some circumstances, yes. But it didn't harm Peter Paul and Mary, the Three Stooges, the Andrews sisters, Emerson, Lake and Palmer, the Marx brothers, the Bee Gees, the Three Tenors ... or the three wise monkeys.

Italy recommends:

> **'Peel a fig for your friend, a peach for your enemy.'**

Though it's not clear why. Considering the reputation 'syrup of figs' has, perhaps the reverse might be a better option.

> **'Friends are like fiddle strings – they must not be screwed too tight.'**
> (England)

> 'The ear of the bridled horse is in the mouth.'
> (Italy)

'A trouble shared is a trouble halved.'

But according to *Coronation Street*, a trouble shared is a trouble everyone knows about tomorrow morning.

You hope the visitors will leave soon? So do the Portuguese:

'Visits always give pleasure, if not in the coming then the going.'

But Jean Paul Richter (*Hesperus*, 1795) didn't agree:

'The best moments of a visit are those which postpone its close.'

A proverb attributed to various sources (Greece, China, Denmark, Benjamin Franklin) says:

'Visitors and fish go stale after three days.'

This is only half true, because fish can be kept in ice or in the deep freeze. But that isn't recommended for visitors.

'Many are dead before they die.'
(Spain)

Take your pick

'Silence is golden'

or

'The squeaky wheel
gets the grease.'

'What butter or whisky
doesn't cure, can't be cured.'

(Ireland)

Weather and Gardens

Are we to believe American folklore?

> 'Rain from the East, rains three days
> at least.'

The Spanish are more realistic:

> 'When God wills, it rains with any wind.'

And the folk in Cheshire are even more pragmatic:

> 'Rain has such narrow shoulders it will
> get in anywhere.'

'Milk cannot come
from a male buffalo, nor
butter by churning water.'
(India)

Back in the 1890s, some believed:

'When it storms on the first Sunday in the month it will storm every Sunday.'

It is a little difficult to take this seriously.

'Make hay while the sun shines.'

This can be seen to have two opposing meanings. Either:

Have fun in the sunshine – rather like 'While the cat's away the mice do play.'

Or the intended meaning:

Get to work while the going is good. Use the sunny times to make sure the hay is brought in before the rainy days which might follow.

'The dawn doesn't hurry if you get up earlier.'

(Spain)

Some weather and gardening 'wisdom' from around the world:

'A windy day is not a day for thatching.'

(Ireland)

'A shady lane breeds mud.'

(England)

'The stupidest peasants have the biggest potatoes.'

(Germany)

'The grape is not ripened by the rays of the moon.'

(Italy)

'The frost hurts not weeds.'

(Holland)

'There is no bad weather, only bad clothing.'

(Sweden)

Have they considered tornadoes, blizzards and floods?

'A man with soft ears is sure to get them pulled.'

(Malaya)

Serbo-Croats think that

> 'Man's journey through life is like
> that of a bee through blossom.'

The French disagree:

> 'Life is an onion – one peels it crying.'

From England in the 1660s came:

> 'If you would be happy for a week,
>   take a wife;
> if you would be happy for a month,
>   kill a pig;
> if you would be happy all your life,
>   plant a garden.'

Rather unfairly, this advice rules out Muslims, Jews, most Buddhists, gays and anyone who lives in an apartment.

'Eaten bread is
soon forgotten.'
(Germany)

'There is no rose without thorns.'

This worthy piece of cynicism once indicated certainty that anything pleasant or desirable would bring something problematical with it. But alas, selective garden science has now rendered it out of date, as there *are* now roses without thorns.

'If things are getting
easier, perhaps you're
heading downhill.'
(Africa)

Seasons and Hemispheres:

Saluting the South

Neil Diamond's famous album *Hot August Night* was bought by his fans all over the world – even though its title was perplexing to people in more than forty nations in the southern hemisphere, where August is the middle of winter and the nights are anything but hot. But Neil Diamond is not alone. His record title, although not a proverb itself, draws attention to the fact that the images within many familiar sayings come mainly from the northern hemisphere, and often (quite understandably) refer to seasons which are the complete opposite to those south of the Equator.

So perhaps Neil Diamond's album should be reissued with the new title *Hot February Night* in the

'One may tire of eating tarts.'

(France)

southern hemisphere. Similarly, we could apply a little gentle surgery to a number of sayings and proverbs so that the months are more appropriate to the other half of the world ...

'Mad as a March hare.'

They skip about in fanciful fashion and do 'pretend boxing' because in the northern hemisphere March is their mating season. But hares in the other half of the world have their spring mating six months later. So below the Equator it would make more sense to say:

'Silly as a September hare.'

'Warm September brings the fruit, Sportsmen then begin to shoot.'

But for the south:

'Warm in May will bring the fruit, Sportsmen then begin to shoot.'

'Eating while standing makes one strong.'
(India)

'Upon St David's Day, put oats and barley in the clay.'

St David's Day is 1 March – not a good time for planting in South Africa, Argentina, New Zealand or Australia. Here is an amended version for a southern spring:

'October 3rd St Cyprian's Day, oats and barley in the clay.'

'If it freezes on St Matthias's Day, it will freeze for a month together.'

This is most unlikely in the southern hemisphere, St Matthias's Day being 24 February – the middle of summer. An adjustment of both saint and month is

'Where the road is straight, don't look for a short cut.'

(Russia)

required, and St Thomas's Day falls in mid-winter, 3 July. Thus:

> 'If it freezes on St Thomas's Day, it will freeze for a month together.'

Another wise saw from the north:

> 'November's sky is chill and drear,
> November's leaf is red and sear.'

But in the south, perhaps:

> 'In May the sky is chill and drear,
> Maytime leaf is red and sear.'

> 'Plant your taters when you will –
> they won't come up until April.'

But for half of the world:

> 'Potatoes in September clay,
> harvest them for Christmas Day.'

'Better a red face
than a black heart.'
(Portugal)

'If February gives much snow, a fine
summer it doth foreshow.'

This must be:

'If August weather brings much snow,
a fine summer it doth foreshow.'

'If Candlemas Day be shower and rain,
Winter is gone and will not come again.'

Candlemas Day is 2 February – the hottest part
of summer for half the world. The date should be
reconvened to Saint Gabriel's Day (29 September).

'St Gabriel's Day brings showers and rain,
Then winter's gone, won't come again.'

'The early riser does
not affect the sunrise.'
(Mexico)

'April brings the primrose sweet,
scatters daisies at our feet.'

Preferably:

'October brings the primrose sweet,
scatters daisies at our feet.'

'Ne'er shed a clout 'til May comes out.'

It is not clear whether this ambiguous saying refers to
the May bush coming out in bloom, or the month of
May being finished ('out'). Either way, it won't work for
half the planet. So:

'Wear your woollies near your skin
When the month of May comes in.'

'He who wishes to eat the
kernel must first crack the nut.'
(Italy)

> 'March winds and April showers
> bring forth May flowers.'

No, but:

> 'August winds, October showers,
> bring forth November's flowers.'

> 'January brings the snow,
> Makes our feet and fingers glow.'

South of the Equator, January is definitely summer:

> 'Cold in August brings the snow,
> Makes our feet and fingers glow.'

'When an elephant
steps on a trap —
no more trap.'
(Africa)

Sleep and Rest

In 1795 Goethe clearly enjoyed the hours of darkness:

'Night is the better half of life.'

Saint John disagreed:

'The night cometh, when no man can work.'

(John 9: 4)

To be fair, John was not living in a major modern city, which would grind to a halt without essential workers on night shifts.

Layabeds were first chided in print by the nun Dame Juliana Berners, in the 1496 publication *The Treatise of Fishing with an Angle*:

**'Who soo woll ryse erly shall be holy
helthy and zely [fortunate].'**

**'It is hard with an empty
hand to catch birds.'**

(Germany)

By 1639, in John Clarke's *Paroemiologia Anglo-Latina*, her advice had become:

> **'Early to bed, early to rise, makes a man healthy, wealthy and wise.'**

Most parents ever since have intoned that warning to their teenagers. In Spain they might also say:

> **'If you would acquire fame, let not the sun shine on you in bed.'**

But there's a little bit of leeway for those whose financial tenure is a bit more secure:

> **'He that will thrive must rise at five,
> He that hath thriven may lie till seven.'**

Or in reverse, those whose fortunes have declined are scorned with:

> **'They can't rise early that used to rise late.'**

The Irish have a more optimistic view:

> **'Good luck beats early rising.'**

> **'He who cannot cut bread evenly cannot get on well with people.'**
> (Czech)

Most famous of all is the proverb:

'The early bird catches the worm.'

This first surfaced in print in 1605, when William Camden described it as a 'proverb' ('The early bird catcheth the worm') in his *Remains Concerning Britain*, so it must have been well known by then. It is obviously intended as advice – an admonition to act quickly without delay, and to take opportunities as soon as they present themselves. The proverb is of course a statement of fact: the early bird does catch a worm. But so does the second bird, and the third and fourth. Birds eat all day, and worms worm around all day, so it isn't always essential – and sometimes not even wise – to make quick decisions, because another worm is quite likely to come along. Besides, consider the alternative: 'Fools rush in where angels fear to tread.'

And by the way, nocturnal birds – owls, kiwis, etc. – get up and eat when night falls and have survived for thousands of years.

'If envy were a ringworm we would all have scabs.'
(Mexico)

Of course, all this advice about early rising pre-dates the invention of all-night television, which wants people to stay up during the dark hours, so that they see more commercials.

One school of thought from the 17th century equates diet with financial success:

> **'Sleep without supping and wake without owing.'**

But a traditional Italian version has a slightly different take:

> **'He who goes to bed supperless tosses all night.'**

> **'Three women, three geese and three frogs make a fair.'**
> (Germany)

In 800 BC, Homer, who must either have been easily bored or perhaps saw sin in inactivity, decreed:

'Too much rest becomes a pain.'

By 1648 the pace of the working world must have increased, causing Robert Herrick to pronounce:

'Labour is held up by the hope of rest.'

But then Thomas Carlyle announced unequivocally in 1830:

'Rest is for the dead.'

Or if not dead, indecipherable, as Aristotle said in 340 BC:

'When they are asleep you cannot tell a good man from a bad one.'

'Keep one eye on the frying pan, the other on the cat.'
(Spain)

Oddities

'Not all are asleep
who have their eyes shut.'

(Italy)

'All who snore are not asleep.'

(Denmark)

'He who sleeps well
does not feel the fleas.'

(Italy)

'The more you sleep, the less you sin.'

(Russia)

'Only stretch your foot to the length
of your blanket.'

(Afghanistan)

'When one begins to turn in bed
it is time to turn out.'

(Ireland)

Sin

When the Countess of Salisbury's garter fell down in 1348, King Edward III chided those who sniggered and founded the Order of the Garter, with the motto:

'Evil be to him who evil thinks.'

This relates to a pious Hebrew maxim, which later seemed to have been on President Jimmy Carter's mind:

'Sinful thoughts are even more dangerous than sin itself.'

No comment from Hugh Hefner or *Playboy* readers.

Italy presents a conveniently liberal view:

'A sin concealed is half pardoned.'

'A small fish can make a big river muddy.'
(Japan)

It's doubtful that the Pope would agree with that, or with:

'Sin undetected is sin absolved.'

Germany proposes a much stricter application:

'Not to be ashamed of sin is to sin double.'

But there is comfort from Poland, where an old belief is:

'Even a saint sins at least seven times a day.'

A complex piece of international law revolves around a situation where 'choice of action' involves an assessment of several differing 'evils', with the admonition:

'Of evils choose the lesser.'

Choosing the 'lesser' did not please Charles Spurgeon, the eminent Victorian Baptist preacher, who advised: 'Of two evils, choose neither.' Mae West did not agree.

**'Grass fears the frost,
frost fears the sun.'**
(China)

Her attitude was: 'Whenever I have to choose between two evils, I always like to try the one I haven't tried before.'

The Old Testament states:

'Rebellion is the sin of witchcraft.'

(1 Samuel 15: 23)

This seems unduly restricting. Causes like women's suffrage and equality for African-Americans had obstacles enough without this biblical dismissal of their actions.

'Experience is a comb
often given by nature
after we are bald.'
(Belgium)

Take your pick

'Never look a gift horse
in the mouth'

or

'Beware of Greeks
bearing gifts.'

'Example is the greatest
of all seducers.'

(France)

Old and New

John Clarke's *Paroemiologia* (1639) stated confidently:

> **'What is new cannot be true.'**

And this view is supported by a proverb from Poland:

> **'Old truths, old laws, old boots, old books
> and old friends are the best.'**

American philosopher Ralph Waldo Emerson in 1841
was doubtful:

> **'Nature abhors the old.'**

King James I didn't agree. English lawyer John Selden
tells us the king used to call for his old shoes – they
were easiest for his feet. He might therefore have
endorsed this African proverb:

> **'New cloth is not new for long, but it is
> old for long.'**

> **'Every sheep is
> suspended on its own heels.'**
> (Egypt)

But the Bible cuts the ground from beneath any innovation:

'There is no new thing under the sun.'

(Ecclesiastes 1: 9)

And in 1775 Queen Marie Antoinette's milliner, the unexpectedly predictive Mme Bertin, claimed:

'There is nothing new save that which has been forgotten.'

It is hard to reconcile the rulings of Ecclesiastes, Mme Bertin, King James I and Ralph Waldo Emerson with the fact that none of them knew about cell phones, BlackBerries, jet travel, polyester and HD television.

Perhaps Geoffrey Chaucer's neat summation in *The Squire's Tale* (1386) was the most accurate:

'By nature, men love newfangledness.'

And that's a thought firmly believed by Apple, Microsoft, Amazon and Vodafone.

'He that lies on the ground can fall no lower.'

(Germany)

In 1756, Benjamin Franklin gloomily warned:

'Tomorrow never comes.'

But an alternative and more optimistic version had been gaining ground. William Hazlitt's version of the Spanish tale of *Calisto and Melibra* (c. 1520) contained the observation that

'Tomorrow is a new day.'

Which hovered in the shadows until Margaret Mitchell penned the final line of *Gone with the Wind* (1937), with Scarlett O'Hara's determined announcement:

'Tomorrow is another day.'

But in the same vein as 'Never do today what you can do tomorrow' (and its cousin, 'Never do tomorrow what you can put off tomorrow') comes this cynical wisdom from Spain:

**'Tomorrow is often the busiest day
of the week.'**

**'Fools and scissors
must be carefully handled.'**
(Japan)

Take your pick

'If at first you don't succeed,
try, try again'

or

'There's no point in flogging
a dead horse.'

'Nobody gathers firewood
to roast a thin goat.'
(Kenya)

First or Second?

Two literary heavyweights offer widely differing views on the wisdom of taking notice of anything (or anyone) at first sight. In c. 428 BC, Euripides opined that

'Second thoughts are the wisest.'

But over two millennia later in 1700, William Congreve had come to a different conclusion:

'First impressions are the most lasting.'

This certainly applies if the first impression is made by the front end of one car on the back end of another.

There are others who subscribe to the truth of the Congreve proverb, but clearly Jane Austen was not of their number. Euripides could not have known about

**'All feet tread not
in one shoe.'**
(Holland)

Elizabeth Bennet and Mr Darcy, but he accurately predicted that Miss Bennet would see the wisdom of revising her initial opinion. And ancient Rome was in agreement:

> 'The first appearance deceives many.'

In 1580 Lyly's *Euphues* observed that

> 'The last dog oftentimes catcheth the hare.'

But by 1670 others had turned the observation on its head:

> 'The foremost dog catcheth the hare.'

> 'Govern a family as if cooking a small fish: gently.'
> [China]

Remedies

Hippocrates, the 'father of medicine', took a cautious approach to problems in 400 BC:

> 'To do nothing is sometimes
> a good remedy.'

Ancient Latin held that

> 'Anceps remedium est melius
> quam nullum.'

> 'A doubtful remedy is better
> than none.'

John Lydgate's *Daunce of Macahabree* (c.1430) stated:

> 'There is a remedy for everything
> but death.'

'One finger can't
lift a pebble.'
(Native American)

But by 1651 confidence had grown. George Herbert, in *Jacula Prudentum*, announced:

> **'There is a remedy for everything,**
> **could men find it.'**

We wish him good luck in finding the remedy for death.

> **'An apple a day keeps the doctor away.'**

It can't do any harm, but proteins, carbohydrates and vitamin B are not just unnecessary whims ...

> **'Laughter is the best medicine.'**

There is little doubt that laughter engenders a feeling of goodwill, which is believed to aid the unwell towards recovery. But regarding it as the 'best' medicine is possibly an overstatement. It would be unwise to give up the antibiotics.

> **'A person born to be**
> **a flowerpot will not go**
> **beyond the porch.'**
> (Mexico)

Richard Taverner's *Proverbs* in 1539 told us:

'Time cures all things.'

But again, antibiotics are a great help...

The Chinese believe:

'Get the coffin ready and watch the sick man recover.'

Seneca (c. AD 60) put forward the belief that

'Tam miser est quisque quam crediti.'

'A person is as downcast as he believes he is.'

'A dry finger
cannot pick up salt.'
(China)

Over many centuries this was modified by bringing 'age' into the equation, and 1871 saw the first publication of the now 'developed' proverb as:

> **'A man is as old as he feels**
> **himself to be …'**

This simply isn't true. A person may be under some delusion about being the age they 'feel', but the unwelcome attentions of arthritis, osteoporosis, baldness, irritable bowel syndrome and other ailments will come calling anyway. No matter how old a person 'feels', when the passport says it's right, they will get a free bus pass.

The proverb also developed a mean-spirited second half:

> **'… and a woman is as old as she looks.'**

> **'Feasting with friends**
> **is good – but not from**
> **the same plate.'**
> (Yiddish)

Death

We spare hardly a thought for what kind of existence we had *before* we came into the world, and it may be just as pointless wondering what will happen when we leave. Greek philosopher Epicurus said c.200 BC:

'Death is nothing to us – since when we are, death has not come, and when death has come, we are not.'

'Dead men tell no tales.'

That used to be the case – until the discovery of DNA.

'The best manure is under the farmer's shoe.'
(Denmark)

'Never speak ill of the dead.'

Unless you can make a profit by spilling some dirt and writing a tell-all biography about them.

'The good die young.'

Some do, others don't. Think The Queen Mother, Sir Edmund Hillary, Mother Teresa, Nelson Mandela ...

'Call no man happy until he dies.'

This rather depressing proclamation originated from the ancient Greek lawmaker Solon, but was brought into prominence centuries later by a situation of genuine sadness. Canadian medical academic Sir William Osler's son was killed at war in 1917, a blow which haunted Osler for the rest of his life. Although successful in many fields, the continuing grief over his lost son caused him to quote the pessimistic Greek proclamation that only death would release him from personal sorrow.

'The fart of a quiet person stinks most.'

(Japan)

From 1670 comes a proverb whose significance – if any – is hidden behind a truth so banal it's hard to take it seriously as 'wisdom':

'They who live longest must die at last.'

There is also a piece of fairly obvious wisdom within Italian tradition:

'Death will find me alive.'

Well, of course it will!

And in 1818 Napoleon faced up to the truth:

'When we are dead we are dead.'

'In an ant colony one drop of dew is a flood.'
(Iran)

In the 17th century, it was believed that

'Death squares all accounts.'

But John Heywood's *Proverbs* (1546) allowed disillusion from someone unpaid after a bereavement, for to get even the smallest payment would be like trying to

'Get a fart of a dead man.'

'Old soldiers never die.'

Like everyone, old soldiers do eventually die. But nations, communities and cultures ensure that respect for them is maintained. Memorials and commemorations form continuing reminders of the value of soldiers' contributions. The sacrifices and courage of old soldiers are preserved in spirit and in stone, and honouring them does not die.

'He who has a straw tail is in fear of its catching fire.'

(Italy)

'A green Yule makes a fat churchyard.'

In parts of Britain, there was for centuries a belief that if the winter weather at Christmas ('Yule') was not as freezing as usual, then germs which normally could not combat cold weather would remain active long enough to cause illnesses among the weak and elderly, and therefore unavoidable deaths during the rest of the season.

This rather morbid proverb dates from 1813, and refers to a person who has died and is about to be buried:

'He is going to grass with his teeth upwards.'

'A dwarf on a giant's shoulder sees farther of the two.'
(*Jacula Prudentum*, 1651)

From the Bible:

'Let the dead bury the dead.'

(Luke 9: 60)

Which, to say the least, is cryptic.

A note of hope from Benjamin Franklin:

**'Fear not death, for the sooner we die
the longer we shall be immortal.'**

'Flatterers are
cats which lick before
and scratch behind.'

(Germany)

Take your pick

In 1532, John Frith's treatise *A mirrour or glasse to know thyselfe* introduced the world to the phrase 'holdeth their noses so hard to the grindstone', which became:

'Keep your nose to the grindstone.'

American singer Mac Davis didn't entirely agree. He was told by band leader Doc Severinsen of a proverb heard from a physician – and in 1974 Mac Davis sang it to acclaim:

'Stop – and smell the roses.'

'A fool looks for dung
where a cow never browsed.'
(Africa)

Oddities

'There is no dying by proxy.'

(France)

'After death no pleasure remains.'

(Italy)

'Death is never at a loss
for occasions.'

(Greece)

'Our last garment is made
without pockets.'

(Italy)

'At birth we bring nothing;
at death we take nothing away.'

(China)

'No man knows fortune until he dies.'

(Netherlands)

'Six feet of earth make us all equal.'

(Italy)

And an American proverb:

'Cemeteries are filled with people
who thought the world could not
get along without them.'

'Wise men make proverbs – and fools repeat them.'

From Samuel Palmer's
Moral Essays on Proverbs (1710)

Sources

Proverbs and wise sayings have been recorded for several thousand years. By the middle of the 16th century, volumes of proverbs had begun to be published in English. Since then, countless collections have appeared in print. Among the comprehensive anthologies consulted for this book are:

G. L. Apperson (ed), *The Wordsworth Dictionary of Proverbs*, Wordsworth Editions, Ware (Herts), 1996.

Julian Baggini, *Should you Judge this Book by its Cover?*, Granta, London, 2009.

Anne Bertram (comp), *NTC's Dictionary of Proverbs and Clichés*, National Textbook Company, Chicago, 1993.

Jonathan Law, *The Penguin Dictionary of Proverbs*, Penguin Books, London, 2000.

Marin H. Manser, *Facts on File Dictionary of Proverbs*, Checkmark Books, New York, 2002.

H. L. Mencken, *Dictionary of Quotations*, William Collins, London, 1982.

David Pickering, *Cassell's Dictionary of Proverbs*, Cassell, London, 2001.

Ronald Ridout and Clifford Witting, *The Macmillan Dictionary of English Proverbs Explained*, Macmillan, London, 1995.

J. Speake (ed), *The Oxford Dictionary of Proverbs*, Oxford University Press, Oxford.

Jon R. Stone, *The Routledge Book of World Proverbs*, Routledge, New York, 2006.

Gregory Titelman, *Random House Dictionary of America's Popular Proverbs and Sayings* (second edition), Random House, New York 2000.

WHO SAID THAT *FIRST*?

The curious origins of common words and phrases

Believe it or not, this may well be the only book to attempt to identify the original sources of common expressions. We might think we know who first said *famous for fifteen minutes*, *annus horribilis*, *the cold war* and *let them eat cake*. A *no brainer*, you might say, but Max Cryer has a surprise or two in store for you. *I kid you not*. In this very readable book, he explores the origins of hundreds of expressions we use and hear every day – and comes up with some surprising findings. Never *economical with the truth*, he might just have *the last laugh*.

Written in Max Cryer's delightfully witty style, *Who Said That* First? is a wonderful book to dip into or settle a friendly dispute. Remember, good books are *few and far between*, and *you get what you pay for*. So *go ahead, make my day*.

EXISLE
PUBLISHING

www.exislepublishing.com

LOVE ME TENDER

The stories behind the world's favourite songs

Some of the world's best-loved songs have had remarkable origins. Had Robert Burns not heard an old man sing a quavering version of an ancient Scottish country song, we would never have had 'Auld Lang Syne'. Miss Jane Ross wrote down the tune she heard played by a piper at an Irish village fair in 1855. Thanks to her, generations of people around the world have been able to enjoy 'Danny Boy'. An old melody composed by a long-dead Mexican street musician was presented to Mario Lanza with new words, and it became his most famous recording: 'The Loveliest Night of the Year'.

Love Me Tender tells the enthralling stories behind 40 popular and traditional songs. Some evolved from folksongs, some are from musical theatre, while others hit the mark because a particular recording appeared at just the right time. In some cases, one word made all the difference: Paul McCartney composed a tune but could only think of the words 'scrambled eggs' to fit it, but fortunately he later came up with the perfect solution: 'Yesterday'. In a book full of surprises and curiosities, Max Cryer reveals stories from all around the world, featuring artists as diverse as Bing Crosby, Judy Garland, Elton John and Marlene Dietrich.

EXISLE
PUBLISHING